SERMON OUTLINES &
ILLUSTRATIONS FOR
EVERY OCCASION

SERMON OUTLINES & ILLUSTRATIONS FOR EVERY OCCASION

Willie W. White

College Press Publishing Company, Joplin, Missouri

Library of Congress Catalog Card Number: 88-071158
International Standard Book Number: 0-89900-306-0

Dedication
To Doris

Table of Contents

Index of Subjects

PREFACE

Twenty-seven years ago *Fifty-two Soul-winning Sermon Outlines and Fifty-two Windows to Lighten Them* came from the press. The reception was gratifying and overwhelming. Throughout the intervening years this little book of sermon outlines and illustrations has been used extensively by preachers, teachers, Bible students, and the "average" members of our churches. Young ministers, particularly, have been aided in sermon preparation and with illustrative materials for teaching and preaching.

The author has been in the preaching ministry for fifty-four years, most of which have been devoted to the blessed work of evangelism. Materials contained in this volume have been used extensively in evangelistic crusades and in located ministries. After such a span of years it is manifestly impossible to indicate the source of many of these materials. I am indebted to many publications and individuals.

This volume goes forth with an earnest prayer that it may not only be inspirational to the reader, but that it may be used in reaching many precious souls for our Lord and nurturing them in "the faith which was once for all delivered unto the saints."

—The Author

HOW TO USE THIS BOOK

1. In sermon preparation.

Some of the outlines you may be able to use "as is," by putting your own "meat" on the skeleton. Other outlines may suggest a different topic or different approach to your own sermon. The illustrations are especially designed for use with the outline.

2. As a study guide.

You will find many of these outlines suitable for Bible studies or suggestive in preparing devotional talks, etc.

3. As an illustration book.

The Subject Index of Illustrations will assist you in locating illustrations or poetry which you may desire to use with specific messages or studies.

4. As a devotional and inspirational guide.

The outlines should prove suggestive for further study and the poems and illustrations should be a source of encouragement and inspiration.

Remembering that "all work and no plagiarism makes a dull speech," and that "He who never quotes is seldom quoted," I send forth this volume. It is yours. Use it to the glory of God.

EVANGELISTIC

EVERYMAN EVANGELISM

Text: Acts 1:8.
INTRODUCTION:
>Do you, more than anything else in the world, want to win souls to Jesus Christ?
>
>Every person you will meet today is going to spend eternity in heaven or in hell.
>
>Several years ago in Vietnam a training conference was conducted for Christian "laymen." Above the speaker's platform, in bold, red, Vietnamese characters, were the words, EVERY LAYMAN AN EVANGELIST, SPREADING THE GOOD NEWS." Attention was centered on three large posters. Let us look at them in the light of our text.

PROPOSITION: ACTS 1:8 IS A DIVINE CALL TO EVERYMAN EVANGELISM.

I. On one side of the auditorium a map of the world with a gleaming cross shedding its rays of light upon Vietnam, beneath the picture the question, **IF NOT HERE, WHERE?** . . . "And ye shall be my witnesses BOTH IN JERUSALEM. . . ."
   1. If not in America, where?
   2. If not in your own state, where?
   3. If not in your own home town, where?

II. On the other side of the auditorium a picture of a Vietnamese man and wife approaching a neighbor's door and, superimposed over the background, the challenge, **IF NOT YOU, WHO?** . . . "And YE shall be my witnesses. . . ."
   1. The Lord meant you when He commanded, "Go ye into all the world."
   2. There ought be nothing unnatural in personal evangelism.
   3. You can reach those the "professional" can not.

III. The third picture in the conference hall depicted a giant clock with the hands standing at five minutes until twelve and above the clock the ominous question, **IF NOT NOW, WHEN?** . . . "But ye shall receive power WHEN THE HOLY SPIRIT IS COME UPON YOU: and ye shall be my witnesses. . . "
   1. The world situation demands that we act NOW.

2. The national situation demands that we act NOW.
3. The personal situation demands that we act NOW. Luke 19:10.

CONCLUSION:

Let witnessing become your magnificent obsession.

May the light of the cross fall upon your community, revealing you and your wife approaching your neighbor's door, motivated by the great world clock, with the hands standing at five minutes until twelve!

THE TAMING OF A MADMAN

He was a great, hulking brute of a man, that madman of Gadar. The fearful villagers had bound him often with fetters and chains, but he had broken them like tow. The legion of demons who possessed him had driven him into the mountains and the tombs, where he had his dwelling. Tormented by the devil, he had stripped off his garments and was continually crying out and gashing his body with stones. . . .

But one glorious day he met the Great Physician. The Master came and touched him, and the next time we see him who had been the madman he is calm and clothed and in his right mind, sitting at the feet of Jesus.

The time arrived that the Teacher must go on about His ministry and, as He was entering the boat, the one who had been the madman besought Him, "Jesus, could I go with you?"

"No," tenderly replied the Master, "I want you to go to your home and to your friends, and tell them what the Lord has done for you."

Oh, can we do it? Will we do it? We who have experienced that healing touch of the Great Physician. Go to your home and to your friends, and tell them what the Lord has done for you!

Just how far am I willing to go
That the Gospel may be preached?
Just how much am I willing to give
That the lost ones may be reached?

EVERYMAN EVANGELISM

Just how much am I willing to pray
For the souls that are lost in sin?
Just how much am I willing to do
To go and bring them in?

Just how yielded am I to Christ?
Do I let His spirit fill?
Just how willing to pay the price—
To obey my Master's will?

COMMISSIONED

Text: Matt. 28:18-20

INTRODUCTION:

We meet together today because someone was an evangelist. What of the generations to come?

Each generation of the church is just one generation from extinction.

God had an only Son, and He was a physician and an evangelist.

His mission on earth: "For the Son of man came to seek and to save that which was lost" (Luke 19:10).

His last expressed desire for His followers: "Go . . . and make disciples" (Matt. 28:19).

If you have never brought a soul to Him you have disobeyed an explicit command of your Lord, you are living a sub-normal Christian life, and you have missed the Christian's highest joy.

PROPOSITION: THREE QUESTIONS YOU MUST ANSWER BEFORE YOU WILL FULFILL YOUR COMMISSION.

I. Make disciples — WHY SHOULD I?
1. Because your Lord asked you to.
2. Because of the state of a soul without the Saviour: "Lost."
3. Because of the changes Christ can bring — II Cor. 5:17
4. Because the love of Christ constrains us — II Cor. 5:14.

II. Make disciples — HOW CAN I?
1. Preach a sermon in shoes — Acts 4:13.
2. Expose souls to gospel preaching — I Cor. 1:21.
3. Speak a good word for Jesus — John 1:42.
4. Every person we meet will spend eternity in heaven or in hell. Speak and act accordingly.

III. Make disciples — WHEN SHALL I?
1. There is but one answer: NOW — II Cor. 6:2.
2. The world situation demands that we act NOW.
3. The national situation demands that we act NOW.
4. The personal situation demands that we act NOW.
   Men need the Saviour, and they need Him NOW.

CONCLUSION:

COMMISSIONED

The highest service you can render to God, to society, or to an
individual is to introduce a soul to Jesus Christ.
There is nothing more needed, more exciting, or more reward-
ing.
"And they that are wise shall shine as the brightness of the
firmament; and they that turn many to righteousness as the
stars for ever and ever" (Dan. 12:3).

I BRUNG HIM

It was Bible School hour in a little rural church in Oregon. Excite-
ment was high, for they were engaged in a contest to bring first-time
guests to Bible School. Seated on the front row was a little, ragged,
dirty-faced urchin. On the seat beside him was another lad, equally
dirty and ragged and nondescript. As soon as the opportunity was
presented the little fellow sprang to his feet, and, tugging at the sleeve
of his friend, he announced proudly in his boyish treble, "This is Jimmy. I brung him!"
Oh please, dear God, when we stand before that Great White
Throne, we, too, can hold someone by the hand and say, "Jesus, this
is Jimmy. I brung him!"

The great world-heart is aching,
Aching fiercely in the night,
And God alone can heal it,
And God alone give light.
Then, they to speak the message,
And to send the living word,
Are you and I, my brother,
And the others who have heard.

but

We grovel among the trifles,
And our spirits fret and toss,
While above us burns the vision
Of the Christ upon the cross;

21

And the blood of Christ is streaming
From His wounded hands and side,
And the lips of Christ are saying,
"Tell my brothers I have died."

THE LOST CHORD

Text: Psalms 51:1-13.

INTRODUCTION:

    Poem, "The Lost Chord," by Adelaide Ann Proctor.

    The Grand Amen is sounded in the heart of man when he gets in tune with God.

    The tragedy is that this chord can become lost.

    David, God's man that he was, lost heaven's harmony from his soul. The harmony was lost by sin — II Sam. 11.

    David pours out his soul for cleansing — Psa. 51.

    When his petition is granted sinners will be converted — Psa. 51: 13.

PROPOSITION: THE KEY TO EVANGELISM IS REVEALED IN PSALMS 51.

  I. GOD'S PEOPLE MUST CONFESS THEIR SIN — verses 2-4.

    1. David did not spare himself nor give soft names to sin — verses 2-3.

    2. David's sin was against God — verse 4.

    3. We prepare for evangelism by confessing our sins — II Chr. 7:14.

  II. GOD'S PEOPLE MUST PRAY FOR PARDON — verse 9.

    1. God has promised to pardon our sin — I John 1:9.

    2. We prepare for evangelism through the pardoning of our sins.

  III. GOD'S PEOPLE MUST PRAY FOR CLEAN HEARTS AND RIGHT SPIRITS — verse 10.

    1. We can not lead others nearer Christ than we ourselves live.

    2. We prepare for evangelism with a clean heart and a right spirit.

  IV. GOD'S PEOPLE MUST PRAY FOR RENEWED FELLOW-SHIP — verse 11.

    1. Evangelism demands the presence of God and power of His Spirit.

    2. We prepare for evangelism through renewing our fellowship with God.

  V. GOD'S PEOPLE MUST PRAY FOR RESTORED JOY — verse 12.

1. Have you lost your joy in the service of the King?
2. We prepare for evangelism through restoration of Christian joy.

VI. GOD'S PEOPLE MUST PRAY FOR A WILLING SPIRIT — verse 12.

1. Are you willing to live for and serve the One Who died for you?
2. We prepare for evangelism through recapturing a willing spirit.

CONCLUSION:

THEN transgressors will be taught and sinners converted — verse 13.

Illus: Franz Schubert's great work, "The Unfinished Symphony," God has an unfinished symphony: the evangelization of the world.

When God's people, with the joy of salvation in their hearts, willingly go into the world with a witness to sinners on their lips, God's unfinished symphony will be completed.

THE LOST CHORD

Seated one day at the organ,
I was weary and ill at ease,
And my fingers wandered idly
Over the noisy keys.

I know not what I was playing,
Or what I was dreaming then:
But I struck one chord of music
Like the sound of a great Amen.

It quieted pain and sorrow
Like love overcoming strife;
It seemed the harmonious echo
From our discordant life.

THE LOST CHORD

I have sought, but I seek it vainly,
That one lost chord divine,
That came from the soul of the organ,
And entered into mine.

It may be that death's bright angel
Will speak in that chord again;
It may be that only in heaven
I shall hear that Grand Amen.

— Adelaide A. Proctor

WHAT KIND OF SINNER ARE YOU?

Text: Romans 3:23; I John 1:8.

INTRODUCTION:

A dirty little word appears 595 times in the Bible; 378 times as a noun, 217 times as a verb: SIN.

Some laugh at sin; some ignore sin; some minimize sin — but sin is. Sin is tragically real. Sin is terrible.

1. Sin is terrible in its nature — it is rebellion against God.
2. Sin is terrible in its consequence — it destroys bodies, homes, society, and it separates from God — Isa. 59:2.
3. Sin is terrible in its penalty — Rom. 6:23. Sin must be forgiven or punished.

Since all "have sinned," and since all "have sin," the question is what kind of a sinner are you?

PROPOSITION: THE ORIGINAL WORDS APPLIED TO TRANSGRESSIONS TELL US WHAT KIND OF SINNERS WE ARE.

I. Rom. 5:12 (*hamartia*) — invariably translated "SIN."

The word that means "to miss the mark."

Illus: A disciple named Judas missed the mark.

II. Rom. 3:23 (*parabasis*) — generally translated "TRANSGRESSION."

The word which means a deliberate violation of the law.

Illus: Josh. 7 — Achan deliberately violated God's law.

III. Rom. 1:18 (*adikia*) — translated "UNRIGHTEOUSNESS," "UNJUST," "INIQUITY."

The word which means evil deeds done to our fellowman.

Illus: II Sam. 11 — King David's sin against Uriah.

IV. Heb. 9:7 (*agnoema*) — translated "ERROR" or "IGNORANCE."

The word which means wrong deeds done in ignorance.

Illus: I Tim. 1:13 — Saul persecuted Christians in ignorance.

V. Rom. 5:9 (*parakoe*) — translated "DISOBEDIENCE."

The word which means failure to hear a command or to listen attentively when God speaks.

Illus.: II Sam. 6 — Uzzah steadying the ark of God.

CONCLUSION:

WHAT KIND OF SINNER ARE YOU?

"All have sinned and fallen short of the glory of God."
There are three things we can do about sin:
1. Welcome it, embrace it, revel in it. Rom. 6:23.
2. Strive alone to overcome it. Rom. 7:24.
3. Accept pardon for sin and power to overcome. Isa. 1:18; I John 4:4.

SOW: REAP

A man rocked a boat to see if it would tip. IT DID!
A laborer stepped on a nail to see if it would go through his shoe. IT DID!
A man looked into a gun to see if it was loaded. IT WAS!
A worker smelled leaking gas and lit a piece of oily waste to find the leak. HE DID!
A young girl kept late hours to see if it really would injure her office work. IT DID!
A man said, "I'll ignore Jesus Christ and see if I go to hell. HE DID!

If you persist in your efforts to overcome sin through your own strength you will be like the Australian Aborigine who obtained a new boomerang, then drove himself crazy trying to throw the old one away.

Man calls sin an accident; God calls it abomination.
Man calls sin a blunder; God calls it blindness.
Man calls sin a chance; God calls it a choice.
Man calls sin a defect; God calls it a disease.
Man calls sin an error; God calls it enmity.
Man calls sin fascination; God calls it fatality.
Man calls sin an infirmity; God calls it iniquity.
Man calls sin a liberty; God calls it lawlessness.
Man calls sin a trifle; God calls it a tragedy.
Man calls sins a mistake; God calls it madness.
Man calls sin a weakness; God calls it wilfulness.
  What do you call it?

"If you don't want the fruits of sin stay out of the orchard."
"If you don't think the wages of sin is death look at the cross."

SAVED FOR SURE

Text: Heb. 7:25.

INTRODUCTION:

The darkest picture ever etched upon the canvas of the centuries is that dark, sordid picture of sin.

The story of sin is almost as old as the story of man.

Relate the story of the temptation and fall. Rom. 5:12.

Because all have sinned all need a Saviour.

What God could have done when man sinned:

1. Wiped out the human race: **justice** without mercy.
2. Granted unconditional pardon: **mercy** without justice.
3. Provided the penaly for sin and the way of pardon.

Only in the cross of Christ do justice **and** mercy meet.

Every individual needs saved from the GUILT, the POWER, and the PENALTY of sin.

PROPOSITION: JESUS, ALONE, IS ABLE TO SAVE FROM THE GUILT, POWER, AND PENALTY OF SIN.

I. JESUS IS ABLE TO SAVE FROM SIN'S GUILT BECAUSE HE OFFERED THE PERFECT SACRIFICE FOR ITS FORGIVENESS.

1. He became sin on our behalf. II Cor. 5:21.
2. There is but one fount of cleansing. Zech. 13:1; I John 1:7.
3. He has provided the remedy. It is adequate. Man must receive it.

II. JESUS IS ABLE TO SAVE FROM SIN'S POWER BECAUSE HE OFFERS POWER TO HELP US OVERCOME.

1. He walked the way before us and thus understands. Heb. 4:15; 2:18.
2. He gives strength to His children. I John 4:4; Phil. 4:13.
3. Paul's secret of overcoming. Rom. 7:25.

III. JESUS IS ABLE TO SAVE FROM SIN'S PENALTY BECAUSE HE EVER LIVES TO MAKE INTERCESSION FOR US (Heb. 7:25).

1. We shall all stand before the judgment-seat of God — Rom. 14:10.
2. Jesus will be our one sufficient attorney — Matt. 10:32.

3. His salvation is "to the uttermost."

CONCLUSION:

Do you have a sufficient attorney? Have you found the One Who is able to save from the guilt, power, and penalty of sin?

Perhaps you may say, "This is all very wonderful, but will God pardon MY sin? Isa. 55:6-7; John 3:16.

Salvation has been provided. It is adequate. Receive it. Be saved for sure.

A SUFFICIENT ATTORNEY

Daniel Curry was a mighty man of God who lived in the midwest many years ago. One night he had a dream which became a classic. Daniel dreamed that he died, that he ascended the golden stairway to the gate of heaven, and that he approached the desk where an angel was working on the books. The angel glanced up and asked, "Your name?"

"Daniel Curry," was the timid reply.

The angel turned and searched the records and then responded, "I'm sorry, but I can't find any Daniel Curry."

Daniel was about to turn sadly away when the angel said, "But you may come in and plead your case if you like."

With the speed of light, Curry was whisked before the great white throne. As he stood there, blinded by the effulgence of the glory that emanated from the throne, a voice came from the very heart of the throne, "Daniel Curry, have you always been good?"

No, Daniel Curry had not always been good.

"Daniel Curry, have you always been pure?"

No, Daniel Curry had not always been pure.

"Daniel Curry, have you always been fair and just in your estimate of others?"

Alas, he had not, and he was again about to turn sorrowfully away when he felt by his side a Presence, and the sweetest voice he had ever heard said, "Father, put this man's sins to my account. He was not perfect, but he stood for me, and I am standing for him."

One day I shall stand there with bowed head, guilty before God.

30

But I have an Attorney Who will stand beside me and say, "Father, he was not perfect, but he stood for me, and I am standing for him. Put his sins to my account."

Do you have a sufficient attorney?

THE THEME OF THE BOOK

Text: John 5:39.
INTRODUCTION:

    The book which we call Holy Bible is a library of 66 books, written by more than 40 men from all walks of life, and living in 6 different countries at the time of writing.

    This book was originally written in three languages, and written over a period of some sixteen hundred years.

    This book contains practically all forms of literature: orations, sermons, letters, poetry, parables, proverbs, etc.

    Yet this book has but one theme: "These are they which bear witness of me" (John 5:39).

PROPOSITION: THE THEME OF THE GREATEST BOOK IS HISTORY'S GREATEST PERSON.

I. THE THEME OF THE OLD TESTAMENT: SOMEONE IS COMING.
   1. The virgin-born seed of a woman — Gen. 3:15; Isa. 7:14.
   2. The divine ruler — Isa. 9:6-7; Micah 5:2.
   3. The suffering, serving sin-bearer — Isa. 53:3-6.

II. THE THEME OF THE GOSPELS: SOMEONE IS HERE.
   1. He is the stable-born king — Matt. 2:1-2.
   2. He is the matchless teacher — John 7:46.
   3. He is the miracle-worker — Matt. 11:4-6.
   4. He is the crucified and risen Saviour — John 20:26-28.

III. THE THEME OF ACTS: SOMEONE CAME.
   1. He came — and His church was established — Acts 2.
   2. He came — and the way of salvation was opened — Acts 4:12.
   3. He came — and all men may now come to Him — Acts 17:30.

IV. THE THEME OF THE EPISTLES AND REVELATION: SOMEONE IS COMING.
   1. He is coming with the clouds — Rev. 1:7.
   2. He is coming to raise the dead — I Thess. 4:16-17.
   3. He is coming to judge all men — Rev. 20:11-12.
   4. He is coming as king — Rev. 19:11-16.
   Are you ready to meet the king?

CONCLUSION:

The theme of the greatest book is the story of the greatest Person.

Summarize the theme of the book.

May your discovery of the theme of the book lead to the salvation of your soul.

JIM

The minister of a certain church was disturbed about a shabbily dressed old man who came into the church every day at twelve o'clock. He asked the caretaker to keep an eye on him, as some of the church furnishings were quite valuable.

The caretaker watched and, sure enough, at twelve o'clock each day the old man entered the church. The caretaker confronted the visitor and said, "Everyone is welcome in this church, but why do you come here every day?"

"Why, I come here to pray."

"But you don't stay long enough to pray. You go up to the altar at twelve o'clock and then go right away."

"Yes, that's true. I'm not well enough educated to pray a long prayer, but every day at noon I just come in and stand before the altar and say, 'Jesus, it's Jim!' I know he hears me."

Some time later Jim was struck by a car and taken to the hospital. The ward where he was taken had long been a sore spot to the nurses. The men grumbled and complained, but gradually there was a change. The men became contented and cheerful. When a nurse inquired as to the reason one of the men replied, "Why, it's old Jim. He's always so happy and cheerful. You can't be unhappy when old Jim's around."

The nurse crossed over to where Jim lay. His silvery hair gave him an angelic look. His quiet eyes were full of peace. "Well, Jim," she greeted him, "the men say you are responsible for the change in this ward. They say you are always happy."

"Yes, nurse, that I am. I can't help being happy. You see, nurse, it's my Visitor. He makes me happy."

"Your visitor?" The nurse was puzzled. She had always noticed that Jim's chair was vacant during visiting hours. "Your visitor," she repeated, "but when does he come?"

'Every day," Jim replied, the light in his eyes growing brighter. "Yes, every day at 12 o'clock He comes and stands at the foot of my bed. He smiles and says, 'Jim, it's Jesus.' "

THE KING OF KINGS

Text: Rev. 19:11-16.

INTRODUCTION:

> Inscribed on the back of a pulpit in Oregon: "We would see Jesus." Let us see Him today as the King of Kings.
>
> Beloved John was granted the Patmos vision of the King (Rev. 19).
>
> *Illus*: At an early presentation of Handel's Messiah, Queen Victoria stood with bowed head during singing of the Hallelujah Chorus.

PROPOSITION: JESUS OF NAZARETH IS THE KING OF KINGS.

I. HE WAS PROPHESIED AS KING.

> Old Testament prophets foretold the coming of a King: Isa. 9:6-7; Zech. 9:9; Psalms 2:6
>
> The world was not ready to receive the babe of Bethlehem's manger.

II. HE WAS BORN AS KING.

> Matt. 2:1-2,11.
>
> The proffered gifts were kingly gifts.

III. HE LIVED AS KING.

> John 6:15 — the man who refused to be king.
>
> Mark 15:2 "Art thou the King of the Jews? . . . Thou sayest."

IV. HE DIED AS KING.

> His last acts were kingly acts: the triumphal entry, the crown of thorns, the kingly robe, the reed scepter, the introduction, "Behold your king," the title over His head, "The King of the Jews."

V. HE TRIUMPHED AS KING.

> Victorious over the stone tomb.
>
> The announcement of His Kingly authority: "All authority hath been given unto me."

VI. HE IS THE COMING KING.

> The King of John's vision: "King of Kings and Lord of Lords."
>
> Before the coming King every knee shall bow and every tongue confess.

35

CONCLUSION:
How strange were there a king without a kingdom.
"My kingdom is not of this world" (John 18:36).
"Thine is the kingdom, and the power, and the glory"
(Matt. 6:13).
Are you a subject of the King of Kings?
Will you crown Him King of your life?

AN APPOINTMENT WITH THE KING

It was July 12, 1960. I sat in the mammoth civic auditorium in Columbus, Ohio, and listened with rapt attention as the late Edwin G. Crouch, Christian attorney and then president of the great North American Christian Convention, delivered a masterful keynote address on the convention theme, "Jesus Christ is Lord of All."

As he approached the conclusion of this superb presentation, he related the story of an event which had profoundly affected his life. When Edwin was a young man, a frequent visitor in the Crouch home was an elderly ambassador, a man in his seventies, a member of the blue-blooded aristocracy of Pennsylvania. Edwin remembered the old man, seated before the fire, smoking an underslung pipe which had been given him by Charles G. Dawes, as he visited with Edwin's father.

There, before the open fire, the conversation frequently turned to matters of religion, and one night Mr. Crouch told his visitor of the beauty and simplicity of the Restoration Movement, and the old man thoughtfully responded, "Why, that's the church I have been looking for all of my life."

Soon thereafter, on a Lord's Day morning, the old ambassador, clad in formal morning attire, walked down the aisle of the First Christian Church in Johnson City, Tennessee, handed the minister his card: "John Otto Giese," and confessed with his mouth the Lordship of Jesus.

The baptismal service was arranged for Sunday evening, and, following the sermon, the minister retired to the dressing room to prepare for the baptism. There, in full evening dress, stood the old ambassador — tie, tails, white gloves, all the accoutrements. "Why, Mr.

Giese, don't you desire to change?'' inquired the startled preacher.

The old man faced the minister and replied, "Sir, if my appointment tonight were with King George, this is the way I would be dressed. If my appointment were with the president of the United States, this is the way I would appear. And, sir, my appointment tonight is with the King of Kings and Lord of Lords.'' And, in full evening dress, John Otto Giese was buried with his Lord in Christian baptism and raised to walk in newness of life.

> Rise up, O men of God!
> Have done with lesser things;
> Give heart and soul and mind and strength
> To serve the King of Kings.

THE KING IS COMING

Text: Rev. 1:7.

INTRODUCTION:

    Jesus the babe was worshipped as king — Matt. 2:1-2.

    Despite His claims and His kingly life, He was rejected by His subjects — John 18:33-37; 19:1-3,14-19.

    This rejected king is coming again.

    This blessed event is mentioned more than 300 times in the 260 chapters of the New Testament. One verse in every 25 refers to His coming again.

PROPOSITION: THE KING IS COMING. PREPARE TO MEET HIM.

  I. THE KING IS COMING.

    John 14:2-3; Acts 1:10-11; I Thess. 4:16; II Pet. 3:10; James 5:7; I John 3:2.

  II. THE KING IS COMING — VISIBLY.

    Acts 1:11; Rev. 1:7.

  III. THE KING IS COMING — UNEXPECTEDLY.

    Matt. 24:37-44.

  IV. THE KING IS COMING — TO RAISE THE DEAD.

    I Thess. 4:16-17; John 5:28-29.

  V. THE KING IS COMING — TO JUDGE ALL MEN.

    John 5:22; Acts 17:30-31; Rev. 20:11-15.

  VI. THE KING IS COMING — TO OVERTHROW SATAN.

    Rev. 20:10; I Cor. 15:20-25.

  VII. THE KING IS COMING — TO DESTROY OUR PRESENT HEAVENS AND EARTH.

    II Pet. 3:10-12.

  VIII. THE KING IS COMING — TO REWARD AND TO PUNISH.

    Matt. 25:31-46.

CONCLUSION:

    We shall all stand before the King — Rom. 14:10-12.

    Are you ready for your meeting with the King?

    There is but one way to prepare to meet Him.

      John 14:6; Acts 4:12; Heb. 5:9.

THE KING IS COMING

The market place is empty,
No more traffic in the streets,
All the builders tools are silent,
No more time to harvest wheat;

Busy housewives cease their labors,
In the court-room no debate,
Work on earth is all suspended
As the King comes through the gate.

Happy faces line the hallways,
Those whose lives have been redeemed,
Broken homes that He has mended,
'Those from prison He has freed;

Little children and the aged
Hand in hand stand all a-glow,
Who were crippled, broken, ruined,
Clad in garments white as snow.

I can hear the chariots rumble,
I can see the marching throng,
The flurry of God's trumpets
Spell the end of sin and wrong;

Regal robes are now unfolding,
Heaven's grand-stands all in place,
Heaven's choir is now assembled,
Start to sing Amazing Grace!

Oh, the King is coming!
The King is coming!
I just heard the trumpet sounding
And now His face I see;

39

Oh, the King is coming!
The King is coming!
Praise God, He's coming for me!
                    —Bill & Gloria Gaither

GOLD FROM GOLGOTHA

Text: Luke 23:33-46.

INTRODUCTION:

The most shameful and painful death ever devised by sinful humanity was the "death of the stake." Describe crucifixion. . . . This was the death our Lord chose to die for us.

During the six hours the Galilean hung upon the cross He spoke seven times. Every word was frought with significance. There is gold to be found at Golgotha.

PROPOSITION: MAY THE GOLD FROM GOLGOTHA DRAW AND KEEP US AT THE FOOT OF THE CROSS.

I. FATHER, FORGIVE THEM.

His first word is a prayer.

The One who prayed like that is the One I need and want as my Saviour.

II. TODAY SHALT THOU BE WITH ME.

In the paradise of God it is always today.

On some "today" your eternal life must begin; it will never begin "tomorrow."

III. WOMAN, BEHOLD THY SON. SON, BEHOLD THY MOTHER.

An assignment from the cross meant something to John. We, too, have been given a sacred assignment.

IV. MY GOD, WHY?

The cause of His orphaned cry: II Cor. 5:21.

He became sin. God hid His face. He died of a broken heart.

V. I THIRST.

The cry of a man. The only word which calls attention to Himself.

The Water of Life has drained Himself dry in the fires of Hell.

VI. IT IS FINISHED.

What is finished? His earthly life, the law, atonement for sin. God is now free to love lost men into His eternal kingdom without violating His holy justice.

VII. FATHER, INTO THY HANDS I COMMEND MY SPIRIT.

Not the cry of a defeated victim, but the proclamation of a triumphant victor.

41

If we have been to Calvary we can exult at the end of life's journey, "Father, into thy hands I commend my spirit."
CONCLUSION:
What is your response to Calvary?
Dale Evans Rogers: "All my life I searched for the pot of gold at the foot of the rainbow; now I've found it at the foot of the cross."
There is gold to be found at Golgotha. Claim it for your own!

REMEMBER THE SCARS

Many years ago General John B. Gordon waged a campaign for a seat in the United States Senate. A former army comrade was a part of the voting body that was to decide if his name would be placed in nomination. The two men had been fellow officers, and through the years terrible resentment had developed between them. Everyone knew this man would fight Gordon's bid to become a senator.

As the balloting began, General Gordon felt the intense gaze of the his enemy. He was staring at the ugly scars which gashed the general's face — marks of his willingness to suffer and bleed for a cause he believed in.

Now it was time for the man's vote! All eyes were upon the face of the general. His former comrade was stricken with remorse. He said with great emotion, "I cannot be against him; I had forgotten the scars — I had forgotten the scars!"

Dear reader, look at Jesus on that cross! It's not a picture on an old Sunday-school card. It really happened. Look at the scars.
—there they are on His head, where the thorns punctured His scalp!
—there, see those in His hands, where the nails gored Him?
—there, see the big one in His side where they savagely speared Him?
—there, look where the nails were rammed through His feet!
—there, look at that one — you'll have to look closely — the one in His heart where our sins gouged and tore Him!
I cannot be against Him. I had forgotten the scars — I had forgot-

ten the scars!

— Joe R. Barnett, in the Lookout

Is His blood on your heart
or on your hands?

OUR UNCLAIMED HERITAGE

Text: Acts 2:38.

INTRODUCTION:

How strange and how sad when heirs fail to claim their inheritance.

There is an inheritance available which many have failed to claim.

A legacy available to all was announced when the first gospel sermon was preached: "Repent ye, and be baptized . . . and ye shall receive the gift of the Holy Spirit" (Acts 2:38). Note: not "you may," nor "you can," but "you shall."

There is much confusion concerning the Holy Spirit. The only completely dependable source of information concerning the Holy Spirit is the Bible, which is the Word of the Spirit.

PROPOSITION: MAY WE PERMIT THE WORD OF THE SPIRIT TO ANSWER OUR QUESTIONS CONCERNING THE HOLY SPIRIT.

I. WHO IS THE HOLY SPIRIT?
1. He is a divine Personality, not an impersonal influence. (The Holy Spirit is referred to as "He," not "it.")
2. He is called the Spirit of God, Spirit of Christ, Spirit of Holiness, Spirit of Truth, and Comforter.
3. He is the third Person of the Godhead — Acts 17:29.
   Jesus (on earth) promised, "I will pray the Father (in heaven), and he shall give you another comforter" (John 14:16).

II. WHAT WILL THE HOLY SPIRIT DO FOR US THAT WE SHOULD DESIRE HIM?
1. Convict of sin, thus leading to the Saviour (John 16:8).
2. Make us free from the law of sin and death (Rom. 8:1-2).
3. Aid us in putting to death the deeds of the body (Rom. 8:13).
4. Enable effective prayer (Rom. 8:26).
5. Remind us who we are (Rom. 8:15-16).

III. THEN HOW MAY WE CLAIM OUR INHERITANCE?
1. Luke 11:13. Desire Him. Comply with the conditions. Clean out the rooms. Open the door. Bid Him come in.

44

2. Acts 2:38. The God Who never told a lie nor failed in a promise said, "You do two things, and I'll do two things!" Trust him!
3. Acts 5:32. No right to claim His promises until you love Him enough to obey Him.

CONCLUSION:

Have you claimed your heritage?

If you have closed doors against Him, open the doors, invite Him in.

If you have not complied with His conditions, obey Him now.

God's last invitation is the invitation of the Spirit: Rev. 22:17.

TURN ON THE POWER

The name, Dr. Dennis Pruett, is a familiar name to a great number of twentieth century Christians. Dr. Pruett has proven himself to be an outstanding physician, preacher, missionary, and Christian gentleman. In the summer of 1982 he was one of the missionary speakers at the Wi-Ne-Ma Week of Missions, which is held annually on the Northern Oregon coast. It was in the course of one of these thrilling missionary messages that he related the following gripping incident.

Dr. Pruett was called on to assist in the first open heart surgery ever performed in the state of North Carolina. Preparations were diligently made. The patient was brought in. The incision was made. The heart was removed and placed in Dr. Pruett's waiting hands.

As Dr. Pruett stood there in surgery, the throbbing, life-sustaining organ in his hand, there was a sudden electrical failure and the operating room went dark. Through the darkness rang out the piercing voice of the head surgeon, "Turn on the power! For God's sake, turn on the power!"

The God-man of Galilee, just before returning to the Father, made a wonderful promise to the little band of disciples: "And ye shall receive power when the Holy Spirit is come upon you. . . ." For God's sake, and for the sake of dying humanity, let's turn on the power!

45

Peacher Paul greeted the disciples at Ephesus (Acts 19) with a question. It was not "Do you attend church?" or "Are you a church member?" or "Have you been baptized?" but "Did you receive the Holy Spirit when ye believed?" And they said unto him, "Nay, we did not so much as hear whether the Holy Spirit was given."

And I fear that these Ephesian disciples were not the only ones who have not heard whether the Holy Spirit is given. If the Spirit abruptly ceased His work today there are many professing Christians who would scarcely know the ifference! What have you done today that you could not have done without the Holy Spirit in your life?

"We should be so filled with the Holy Spirit that if a mosquito should bite us he would go away singing, 'There is Power in the Blood!!!' "

WHEN GOD CLOSES THE DOOR

Text: Gen. 7:16.
INTRODUCTION:

    God instructs Noah to build an ark — Gen. 6.

    Noah willingly complies — "Thus did Noah."

    Sinful humanity is warned.

        Noah "a preacher of righteousness" — II Pet. 2:5.

    The door of the ark stood open during God's period of grace.

        He is "not willing that any should perish" (II Pet. 3:9).

    The flood comes. Noah's family and the animals enter the ark.

    God closes the door.

    When God closes the door it is too late to be saved.

PROPOSITION: THERE ARE BUT THREE TIMES IN HUMAN EXPERIENCE WHEN GOD CLOSES THE DOOR.

I. Matt. 25:10 — THE BRIDEGROOM RETURNED — AND GOD CLOSED THE DOOR.

    1. The bridegroom will return.

        Jesus promised it. Angels declared it. Apostles preached it.

    2. The manner and purpose of His return. Acts 1:11; Matt. 25:31-46.

    3. Our attitude and conduct while we wait His return — II Pet. 3:10-12. Expectancy, activity, purity.

II. Matt. 27:3-5 — JUDAS DIED APART FROM CHRIST — AND GOD CLOSED THE DOOR.

    1. There is nothing more certain about life than death — Heb. 9:27.

    2. It is too late to be saved when God closes the door in death — II Cor. 5:10.

    3. Then common sense calls us to prepare for death NOW — II Cor. 6:2.

III. Matt. 12:31-32 — THEY BLASPHEMED THE HOLY SPIRIT — AND GOD CLOSED THE DOOR.

    1. There is but one sin which cannot be pardoned. There is no specific sin for which the blood of Christ can not atone.

    2. The reason blasphemy of the Spirit can not be pardoned is that the blasphemous heart has become so hardened that

the merciful God can not get in. Gen. 6:3; Hosea 4:17; John 12:39; Rom. 1:24,26,28.

3. This door has not closed upon man as long as he desires to repent, for this desire would indicate the striving of the Spirit.

CONCLUSION:

19½ centuries ago God opened a door: the door of salvation. Throughout the years the door has stood open. In the doorway stands the God-man of Galilee, holding out hands marred by the nails of Calvary's cross, and saying, "Come!"

Come into the ark of safety NOW!

A DERELICT

A good number of years ago, a captain of a whaling vessel off Greenland found himself at night surrounded by icebergs.

As morning dawned, he sighted a ship not far away, and as it is a common practice among whalers long at sea, he ordered a boat lowered and manned, for he wished to board her. He and his crew of oarsmen carefully picked their way through the narrow lanes of open water toward that mysterious-looking craft. Coming along side, he hailed the vessel with a loud, "Ahoy there!" Nothing happened, nobody appeared. He hove to closer and got into a position where he could look into a porthole; and peering in he saw a man, evidently the captain, sitting at a table, apparently writing. He hailed the vessel again, but the figure did not move. He boarded the vessel, went into the cabin and touched the body and found it frozen stiff. Dead! Looking further, he found the crew, frozen, some in their hammocks, others in the cabin; and from the last entry in the log book it actually appeared that this vessel, a floating sepulchre manned by dead men, had been drifting about the Arctic Sea for thirteen years.

Shipmate of mine, I can say with the voice of twenty-two years of experience that there are millions of human souls who have refused God's gift of eternal life by grace through faith in Christ Jesus. Having heard again and again the Gospel message, they closed their hearts against the calling of the Holy Spirit until, at long last, the Spirit could not speak to them.

WHEN GOD CLOSES THE DOOR

They tell us that millions now living may never die, and that may be true for the Lord may come soon; but I say to you on the authority of God's Word, millions now living are already dead, dead in trespasses and sins. They have drifted into the killing regions of arctic darkness and frost. Oh, many of them have the appearance of life, they look as though they were living, like the frozen and the long dead ship's captain sitting at his desk with pen in hand, but their souls are dead. As Jesus said, "Ye will not come to Me that ye might have life."

—First Mate Bob

LEGEND — LIAR — LUNATIC — OR LORD?

Text: Matt. 22:42.
INTRODUCTION:
>   Nearly two millenia ago a babe named Jesus was born. Unusual circumstances attended His birth.
>   He made claims such as no other man ever made. (Summarize.)
>   We must make a choice concerning Jesus of Nazareth. We must accept His claims or cast Him aside completely.
>   Matt. 22:42 — "What think YE of the Christ?" Everything in time and eternity is dependent upon your answer.

PROPOSITION: JESUS OF NAZARETH IS LEGEND, LIAR, LUNATIC, OR LORD.

I. JESUS IS NO LEGEND.
   1. The Bible declares Him a character in history. Acknowledge the historicity of Jesus or explain away the Bible.
   2. History declares He is not a legend. (Testimony of historians and church fathers).
   3. The calendar declares He is not a legend. When you write the date you confess His birth.
   4. Disbelievers declare Him a historic character. Document. . . .

II. JESUS IS NO LIAR.
   1. How could a liar work miracles, change lives, and give teaching never surpassed?
   2. Why would a liar go to a cross for his lie?
   3. How could a liar triumph over the grave?

III. JESUS IS NO LUNATIC.
   1. His teaching was not that of a madman. "Never man so spake."
   2. His power was not that of a madman.
   3. His prophecies were not those of a madman.

IV. THEN JESUS MUST BE LORD. John 13:13.
   1. His life was the life of God. John 14:9.
   2. His words were the words of God. John 14:24.
   3. His works were the works of God. John 10:37-38.

CONCLUSION:
What think YE of the Christ?
He is no legend, no liar, no lunatic. Then He must be deity incarnate, God humbling Himself to redeem His lost creation. If this be true, how we ought fall down at His nail-pierced feet in faith and adoration, as we cry out, "My Lord, and my God."

MY LORD AND MY GOD

It was an exciting evening in old Jerusalem. Disciples were cowering behind closed doors for fear of their enemies when suddenly the Master, Whom they had seen crucified, stood in the midst, with the old familiar greeting, "Peace be unto you." And they were glad when they saw the Lord.

As John tells the story, he interjects this sad comment, "But Thomas was not with them when Jesus came." Here is a disciple who had "quit going to church," and what a blessing he missed! The other disciples declared, "Thomas, we have seen the Lord. He is alive!"

And Thomas replied, "Oh, no! They crucified my Lord. I saw them drive spikes through hands and feet and thrust a spear into His side. Except I shall see the print of the nails, and put my finger into the print of the nails, and put my hand into his side, I will not believe."

Eight days hurry by and the disciples are within and this time Thomas is with them — and Jesus comes — and He singles out Thomas — and He calls, "Thomas, come here. Thomas, put your finger in the nail prints. Thomas, put your hand into my side; and be not faithless, but believing."

And Thomas cries out, "My Lord and my God."

If He is Who He claimed to be . . . If He is deity incarnate . . . If He is God stooping low to redeem His lost creation . . . If He is the resurrected King . . . How we ought fall prostrate before those nail-pierced feet and cry out in loving subjection, "My Lord and my God."

———

A child, holding her father's hand, stood before W.H. Hunt's great painting and gazed upon it. The look of grief and ill-requited kindness on the worn face of Christ touched her tender heart.

At length, with slowly filling eyes, she asked, "Daddy, did He get in?"

That is the question. On it hang the issues of the Judgment Day. The scriptures plainly teach that when we stand before the Throne of God, the one great question will be, "Did this man accept Christ as His personal Saviour, or not?"

Christ is still saying, "Behold, I stand at the door and knock." Will you let Him in?

MY DAY OF DECISION

Text: Joshua 24:15

INTRODUCTION:

We meet some heroic characters on the pages of the Bible. In the front line stands General Joshua.

Relate story of sending the spies (Numbers 13). Caleb and Joshua bring a good report.

Joshua never wavered; he was always God's man. He led God's people into the Land of Promise.

As an old man, Joshua assembled God's people and issued a challenge: Joshua 24:14-18.

PROPOSITION: WILL YOU MAKE THIS YOUR DAY OF DECISION?

I. THERE IS A CHOICE TO BE MADE: "CHOOSE."
1. God made man a creature of choice. How grateful we ought to be.
2. Of all of life's choices, there is none more important than the one presented by Joshua.

II. THE CHOICE IS: "CHOOSE WHOM YOU WILL SERVE."
1. "The gods beyond the river" — the idols of the Amorites.
2. "Or Jehovah." There was no other choice; no middle ground.

III. THE CHOICE IS PERSONAL: "CHOOSE YE."
1. Some things we must do alone: be born, die, choose.
2. This is one of life's choices which can not be avoided.

IV. THE CHOICE MUST BE MADE NOW: "CHOOSE YE THIS DAY."
1. Tomorrow never comes — II Cor. 6:2.
2. There is danger and death in delay.

V. THE CHOICE DETERMINES YOUR DESTINY AND THE DESTINY OF OTHERS: "AS FOR ME AND MY HOUSE."
1. The power of influence.
2. You cannot decide for others, but your choice will influence others — "We also will serve Jehovah."

CONCLUSION:

This is your day of decision.

What you must do in choosing Christ: I Cor. 1:21; Acts 16:31;

Acts 3:19; Rom. 10:9-10; Mark 16:16.
Will you decide NOW for Jesus Christ?

MY DAY OF DECISION

She was a gracious Christian lady. She was possessed by a winsome personality and had many abilities, but was controlled by a Christ-like humility. Among her many abilities was that of being able to write beautiful poetry. She frequently penned verse which brought satisfaction to her and inspiration to others. She was also one who suffered greatly in body, but was patient in suffering and her life was a witness to many.

We were engaged in an evangelistic crusade in her home church and were preparing for a great day of decision and victory for Christ. In the dead of the night verses came to our little sufferer, and she arose and captured them on paper. A short while later this gracious soul slipped away to be with the Lord she loved. Her husband found the words she had penned that night, and handed to me this beautiful testimony:

> This is my day of decision:
> Tomorrow is too far away;
> Yesterday's sunset has faded —
> Sunrise has brought a new day.
>
> This is my day of decision!
> This is the opportune hour;
> I will surrender to Jesus;
> Trust in His wonderful power.
>
> This is my day of decision.
> Father, I thankfully bow,
> And, singing my praises to heaven,
> I begin serving Thee now.
>
> —Pearl Pierson

"Behold, now is the acceptable time; behold, now is the day of salvation."

—II Cor. 6:2

THE LAST WORD FROM HELL

Text: Luke 16:19-31
INTRODUCTION:
>The doctrine of Hell an unpopular doctrine. Gal. 1:10.
>
>Many have given up a belief in Hell, but not because of anything they have found in the Bible.
>
>Only once Jesus spoke describing Heaven; 13 times He warned men of Hell. Was He mistaken? Did He lie? Or is there a Bible Hell?
>
>The last word from Hell is found in Luke 16:19-31.

PROPOSITION: WHAT WE LEARN FROM THE LAST WORD FROM HELL.

I. THE LAST WORD FROM HELL IS THAT LIFE FOLLOWS DEATH — verses 22,23.

>Human reason, nature, and the Word of God declare that life follows death. John 5:28-29; I Cor. 15:52; Rev. 20:12.

II. THE LAST WORD FROM HELL IS THAT HELL IS A PLACE OF SUFFERING — verses 23,24.

>The most terrible words man has coined are used to warn men of hell: "place of outer darkness," "bottomless pit," "lake burning with fire and brimstone," "Gehenna." (Describe valley of Hinnom.)

III. THE LAST WORD FROM HELL IS THAT PRESENT FACULTIES ARE MAINTAINED — verses 24,25.

>In Hades the rich man could feel, see, speak, hear, and remember.
>
>If you go to Hell you will take your conscience with you.

IV. THE LAST WORD FROM HELL IS THAT EARTHLY POSITION DOES NOT DETERMINE ETERNAL POSITION — verse 25.

>The rich man had all that money could buy, but he could not buy off the court of heaven.
>
>The rich man in life became the beggar in eternity.

V. THE LAST WORD FROM HELL IS THAT THERE IS NO SECOND CHANCE — verse 26.

>The great gulf fixed means eternity.
>
>What could God possibly do to cause men to love Him in the

55

next life that He has not already done?

VI. THE LAST WORD FROM HELL IS THE CALL TO REPENTANCE — verse 30.

God would have all men to be saved.

Why heed the divine call to repentance? Fear. Hope. Love.

CONCLUSION:

The last word from Hell ought to direct us heavenward.

If Christ is the one way to pardon; if His way is the best way, the happiest way, the most useful way; if His way is the one way to eternal bliss, what possible reason could you give for refusing Him?

TRUE — OR FALSE?

A young seminary graduate was preaching a trial sermon and decided to assure himself of popularity by declaring "the larger hope" — so he discredited the existence of Hell and expressed himself in terms of Universalism. An elderly Quaker lady waited on him at the close of his discourse and said, "If what thee says is true, we don't need a preacher. If what thee says is false, thee is a liar and thou hast no business in the pulpit!"

Where is Hell? Why it is at the end of a godless life.

SEPARATED

"Too bad about your wife and you," said a minister to a certain man.

"How's that?" asked the man.

"Well, it seems that you and your wife are going to separate," explained the preacher.

"Nonsense!" cried the man, "There is perfect harmony between us; no such thought ever entered our minds."

"Perhaps not," replied the preacher, "But your wife is a Christian and is going to Heaven, while you are without Christ and are headed for Hell."

It is better to be late at the golden gate
Than to arrive in Hell on time.

A king's jester who always enjoyed a practical joke was driving through the English countryside. He spotted a small boy playing and jokingly called out, "I say lad, which is the way to hell?" Possibly the boy misunderstood the question, but without hesitation he replied, "Go straight on, sir; you'll soon be there."

THE LATEST NEWS FROM HEAVEN

Text: Rev. 21:1-4,10-12,21-27; 22:1-5,17.

INTRODUCTION:

The latest news from heaven comes from the pen of John, the beloved.

John, the aged, in the isle of Patmos, for the word of God and the testimony of Jesus.

While in the Spirit on the Lord's Day, the curtain of the centuries was drawn aside, and John was granted the vision of the home his Lord had gone to prepare.

Listen to the latest news from heaven. (Read text.)

PROPOSITION: MAY THE LATEST NEWS FROM HEAVEN WOO US HEAVENWARD.

I. THE LATEST NEWS FROM HEAVEN CONTAINS A DESCRIPTION.

1. It is the description of a beautiful city — 21:2,10-12.
2. It is the description of a comfortable city — 21:3-4.
3. It is the description of a roomy city — 21:16.
4. It is the description of a permanent city — 22:5.

II. THE LATEST NEWS FROM HEAVEN BEARS A WARNING.

1. A warning of impending judgment — 20:11-15.
2. A warning of that which bars from heaven — 21:27.
3. A warning that your name must be written in the Lamb's book of life — 20:27.

III. THE LATEST NEWS FROM HEAVEN ISSUES AN INVITATION.

1. Who invites? 22:17 (the Spirit, the bride, he that hears).
2. Who is invited? 22:17 (he that is athirst, he that will).
3. What is the invitation? 22:17.
   a) "Come" — this blessed word appears 680 times in the Bible.

   God is about to close the Book, but unwilling to close it without one more invitation.
   b) Take the water of life freely. John 4:14.

CONCLUSION:

How interested are you in heaven?

58

Are you so interested in your possessions and pleasures that
you are giving it little thought?
Why wear glass beads when you can have diamonds? Why
play mud pies when you can be building cathedrals?
There is but one road that leads heavenward. John 14:6.
Make heaven your home tonight.

WHERE IS YOUR HOME?

H.C. Morrison went to Africa. He went with but one purpose: to
lead precious souls to the Lord Jesus Christ. As a missionary, Morrison gave himself in sacrificial service for Christ in that dark conti-
nent. After years of faithful service to his Lord, Morrison's health
broke and he was forced to the United States. When he boarded his
ship he discovered that Teddy Roosevelt was on the same vessel.
Roosevelt, also, had been in Africa, hunting lions.

As the ship steamed into New York harbor, it seemed that all of
New York City had turned out to welcome Roosevelt. Horns were
blowing; bells were ringing; whistles were tooting; bands were playing;
the mayor was there with his speech of welcome.

H.C. Morrison said, "Broken in body, I stood on board that ship,
the loneliest man in all the world. I had been in Africa, slaving for the
Lord Jesus Christ, and there was not a person in that whole crowd to
welcome me home."

"Then," said Morrison, "suddenly that scene in New York faded
and I said to myself, 'Why should I be worried? I'm not home yet!' "

In his imagination he saw the pearly white city. He heard the
trumpets blow, the bands play, and the angelic choir. He saw the gates
of pearl, and then Gabriel shouted, "Open the gates; H.C. Morrison
is coming home!"

The angels put new robes on him and together they walked down
those golden streets of glory. Then they came to the great white throne
where the King of Kings was seated, and the Lord Jesus stepped down
from His throne, held wide His arms, and said, "Welcome home,
Henry, we've been waiting a long time for you."

Is heaven your home tonight?

WORSHIP

THE PRAYER PERFECT

Text: Matt. 6:5-13.

INTRODUCTION:

    Jesus of Nazareth was a masterful teacher, a peerless preacher, a successful healer, yet His disciples never asked, "Teach us to teach," nor "Teach us to preach," nor "Teach us to heal," but they did petition, "Lord, teach us to pray."

Jesus answered their petition in Matt. 6:5-13.

1. Do not pray to be seen of men. v. 5.
2. Pray an "inner chamber" prayer. v. 6.
3. Do not use vain (idle) repetitions. v. 7.
4. "After this manner pray ye:"

PROPOSITION: THE PRAYER PERFECT EMBODIES PRAISE AND PETITION.

I. PRAISE OF GOD.
    1. "Our Father who art in heaven."
       The first word casts aside all selfishness. "I" or "my" is not found in this model prayer.
       "Father" reminds us of our family relationship.
    2. "Hallowed be thy name."
       His name will not be hallowed (made holy) before men unless we make it so by our speech and conduct.
    3. "Thy kingdom come."
       Dare not so pray then do nothing to extend His kingdom.
    4. "Thy will be done, as in heaven, so on earth."
       In heaven His will is omnipotent.

II. PETITION FOR MAN.
    1. For man's material needs: "daily bread."
       "Bread," the symbol of necessity, not "milk and honey," the symbol of affluence.
       "Daily." Not to ask for tomorrow's bread. Who wants stale bread?
    2. For man's spiritual needs:
       a) "Forgive us our debts."
       To what extent? "As we have forgiven our debtors." vs. 14,15.
       b) For victory over temptation.

Our Lord was "in all points tempted like as we are, yet without sin." (Heb. 4:15).

The same power which enabled Him to overcome is available to us.

CONCLUSION:

This is the model prayer. The Prayer Perfect must embody praise of God and petition for man.

When we learn to so pray we can join the hallelujah chorus, "For thine is the kingdom, and the power, and the glory, forever. Amen."

POTENT PRAYERS

Peter Marshall, late chaplain of the United States Senate, prayed some potent prayers before that distinguished body. His prayers were so disturbing that a colleague once remarked, "I never know whether Peter Marshall is praying for me or at me." The following is a sample of Peter Marshall's prayers.

"O Lord our God, even at this moment as we come blundering into Thy presence in prayer, we are haunted by memories of duties unperformed, promptings disobeyed, and beckonings ignored. Opportunities to be kind knocked on the door of our hearts and went weeping away. We are ashamed, O Lord, and tired of failure. If thou art drawing close to us now, come nearer still, till selfishness is burned out within us and our wills lose their weakness in union with Thine own."

What you say on your knees won't have much effect
unless you practice it on your feet.

A LITTLE KID'S PRAYER

Perhaps I ain't religious,
But when I say a prayer,
I sorta feel inside o' me
That God is always there.

THE PRAYER PERFECT

Perhaps I don't exactly
   Know fancy words to say,
But I'm real sure God understands
   When I jest try to pray.

I guess God always listens
   'Cause His own child, you see,
Was Jesus, who was once a boy —
   A little kid like me.

So maybe words don't matter
   If God is in my heart.
I'm pretty sure He likes to hear,
   An' take a feller's part.

If you won't talk to God on a clear day
there isn't much use to yell at Him in a storm.

Prayer is a golden river by whose brink
Some die of thirst, while others kneel to drink.

THE DAWN BY GALILEE

Text: John 21:1-17.
INTRODUCTION:

    Picture the beautiful Sea of Galilee. Here Jesus had called His disciples. Here He performed much of His ministry.

    What has transpired: death and resurrection of the Son of God; "He goeth before you into Galilee: there ye shall see him."

    Disciples have come again to Galilee. Peter said, "I go a fishing," and his friends responded, "We also come with thee."

PROPOSITION: MAY WE LEARN THE LESSONS THE DISCIPLES LEARNED AT GALILEE.

I. THAT NIGHT THEY TOOK NOTHING — verse 3.

    How discouraging! Every Christian worker knows the feeling of seeing the net come in empty.

    Could it be because they were relying on their own abilities?

II. JESUS STOOD ON THE SHORE WHILE THEY FISHED — verse 4.

    There is no more beautiful picture of God than this: a God Who wants to be partner with man, sharing our joys and our sorrows.

III. WHEN DAY WAS BREAKING JESUS SPOKE — verse 5.

    Why wait until daybreak to speak? It could not have been so important the night before. They have now reached the end of their endurance, now willing to admit their failure.

IV. JESUS FILLED THEIR NETS WITH FISH — verse 6.

    Why? Was He saying that He wanted them to be successful; that He wanted them to depend on Him?

V. JESUS CALLED THEM TO BREAKFAST — verses 9-12.

    How tragic had they been left with the fish. At times we are so busy with the fish that we miss the fellowship.

VI. JESUS REVEALED THE SECRET OF SERVICE — verses 15-17.

    Three times, about a fire of coals, Peter had denied his Lord. Now, three times, about another fire, he reaffirms his love and learns the secret of service: LOVE.

The two words here translated "love". . . . Are we Jesus' friends or do we worship and adore Him?

It is love which sanctifies our service and motivates our ministry.

CONCLUSION:

When we learn these lessons from Galilee His sheep will be fed.

Illus: The story of Tuan (below).

Love Him — Accept Him — Obey Him — Serve Him.

MY SHEEP

The sun rose over the Rhodesian bush, its golden rays penetrating the little straw hut where twelve-year-old Tuan lay sleeping. Tuan was a shepherd of the Shona tribe and, despite his tender years, he had already demonstrated his courage and ability. He awoke with a start to the bleating of his sheep. Springing to his feet, and brushing the dust from his meager clothing, he hurried to the fold where the sheep were already pressing against the gate.

Tuan knew where he would pasture his sheep that day. Some distance away was a meadow where they would find ample pasture and water. The sun beat down mercilessly as Tuan led his charges to pasture, but what a disappointment to find the meadow was filled with cattle and a herdsman, sitting in an ox cart under a baobab tree.

Rather than risk a confrontation, Tuan decided to lead his flock around the meadow to the hillside where they would find springs of water and lush vegetation. He was doing well keeping his sheep from the cattle until a sheep ran up and tried to rub noses with a calf. The mother became agitated and as Tuan tried to separate the two the cow kicked him in the chest.

The sun and the sky swirled and Tuan fell to the ground, losing consciousness. The herdsman, seeing what had happened, hurried to the side of the prostrate form and, noting the blood trickling from his mouth and realizing he must find help, picked up the little shepherd boy and placed him in the back of his ox cart.

Mashoko hospital was twelve miles away and after two hours of bumping over the rocky trail, they arrived at the hospital. Dr. Jerry Smith and Dr. Bob Pruett were on duty. They decided to monitor

67

Tuan's condition, and if it worsened, Dr. Pruett would operate. When vital signs began to deteriorate the boy was moved into the operating room. As the nurse prepared the anaesthetic and oxygen a low moan came from the quiet little figure on the table. Tuan's lips began to move and the nurse bent low to try to catch the words. Tuan's arm dropped over the edge of the table. The little shepherd boy was dead.

Dr. Pruett asked, "Could you make out what he said?"

"Yes," the nurse replied through her tears, "he said, 'My sheep, my sheep, who will feed my sheep?' "

Listen — out there in the distance — can you hear the bleating of the sheep?

HOW TO GROW A CHURCH

Text: Eph. 4:1-16.
INTRODUCTION:

    God wants His church to grow. The kingdom of heaven is like the growth of the mustard seed and the working of leaven (Matt. 13).

    The New Testament church was a growing church: 3,000, then 5,000, then "the number of the disciples was multiplying." 500,000 Christians in 100 A.D.; 2 million in 200 A.D.

    Paul exhorts the Ephesian Christians to build up the church and in Ephesians 4 he tells them how.

PROPOSITION: LET US LEARN PAUL'S SECRET OF CHURCH GROWTH AS REVEALED IN EPHESIANS 4.

  I. WALK WORTHILY — verses 1-6.
    1. How we are to walk: with lowliness, meekness, longsuffering, and forbearance.
    2. What we are to keep: the unity of the Spirit in the bond of peace.
       Unity a fragile quality. We must work carefully to maintain it.
    3. The unity we are to keep has its basis in seven unities — verses 4-6.
       All divisions in the body are the result of violating one or more of these unities.

  II. SERVE FAITHFULLY — verses 7-12.
    1. The grace was given to each one — verses 7-8.
    2. Our gifts differ, but all are for the building up of the body — verses 11-12.
       It is not a question of what we have but what we are doing with what we have that is important.
       Illus: Parable of the talents (Matt. 25).

 III. MATURE LOVINGLY — verses 13-16.
    1. The three-fold goal of verse 13.
    2. Cut out the kid stuff — verse 14.
    3. Maturity is reached through speaking truth in love — verse 15.
       We need not choose between truth and love.

CONCLUSION:
God wants His church to grow; do you?
The church will grow when we who are members learn to walk
worthily, to serve faithfully, and to mature lovingly.
Illus: Committed to the cause (following page).

COMMITTED TO A CAUSE

It is Dr. Frederick Schwartz to whom we are indebted for the
following heart-searching story.

A man in San Francisco was returning home from work at mid-
night when he met on the street a neighbor who was an avowed communist.

"Where are you going at this time of night?" the man inquired of
his neighbor.

"I'm going to a party meeting," was the prompt reply.

"A party meeting? Why, man, don't you know it's mid-night. Will
anyone be there?"

"Those who should be there will be there," came the response.
The communist neighbor went on to explain: "You see, we communists divide our day into thirds. Eight hours are given to making a
living; eight hours are devoted to eating and sleeping; the third eight
hours belong to the party, and we use that time to promote the
cause!"

Small wonder that communism is engulfing the earth! How committed are we to The Cause?

SEVEN PROBLEMS OF THE CHURCH

1. Unbended Knee
2. Unread Book
3. Unattended Church
4. Unpaid Tithe
5. Unrealized Cross of Christ
6. Unpassionate Heart
7. Unconcern for Lost Souls.

If you are not willing to give up everything for Christ
are you willing to be made willing?

MAJORING IN MINORS

Text: Matt. 6:33.

INTRODUCTION:

What is of greatest importance to you? Wealth? Health? Fame? Popularity? Power? Education?

Jesus indicated what ought to be of greatest importance in Matt. 6:33: "Seek ye first his kingdom, and his righteousness."

Many want the kingdom, but don't want it first.

Many pray, "Thy kingdom come — but not now."

The kingdom of God ought to be of major consideration, but many are majoring in minors.

PROPOSITION: LET US LEARN FROM NEW TESTAMENT CHARACTERS WHO MAJORED IN MINORS.

I. THREE WOULD-BE DISCIPLES — Luke 9:57-62.
1. A certain man who put comfort first — verses 57-58.
2. Another who put a loved one first — verses 59-60.
3. Another who put home-ties first — verses 61-62.
4. These would-be disciples put earthly things first: earthly comforts, earthly sorrows, earthly affections.

II. A REALTOR, A FARMER, AND A HEN-PECKED HUS-BAND — Luke 14:15-24.
1. The realtor put his possessions first.
2. The farmer put his business first.
3. The husband put his family first.
4. They either loved these things too much or the master too little.

III. A WOMAN WHO ENTERTAINED THE MASTER — Luke 10:38-42.
1. Martha honored Jesus as guest. Mary honored Him as teacher.
2. It is good to minister to the Master, but to sit at His feet is better.
3. Martha was rebuked because she majored in minors.

IV. A RICH YOUNG RULER — Mark 10:17-22.
1. He was reverent, sincere, and law-abiding.
2. His goodness had been negative — verses 19-20.

71

3. He made the Great Refusal. How many forego their right to heaven for trifles.

CONCLUSION:

The Kingdom of God is divine.

The Kingdom of God is eternal.

The Kingdom of God was purchased with the blood of the Son of God.

Will you seek FIRST His kingdom and His righteousness?

WHO IS GREATEST?

Dr. Mecklenburg was a Methodist preacher who ministered several years ago in Minneapolis, Minnesota. He was a world-traveler, and visited Russia several times between World War I and World War II. In fact, he was in Russia at the outbreak of World War II.

It was during these years that Dr. Mecklenburg was with a party of tourists who were visiting Moscow. Across from Red Square stands a building housing a museum which contains some of the personal effects left by the great Russian novelist, Leo Tolstoi. Among the items on display are manuscripts of his books, furniture from his humble home, and many other items of a personal nature. The Russian guide spoke in glowing terms of the abilities and accomplishments of the novelist.

The party had completed their tour of the museum and had started down the sidewalk, when they heard the sound of a voice calling, "Wait; wait!" They turned to see their guide running down the museum steps toward them.

"I didn't want to leave you with the wrong impression," the guide said breathlessly; "there have been several great men who have lived, and Tolstoi was just one of them."

When questioned by one of the tourists as to who he thought to be the greatest men who ever lived, the Russian thoughtfully responded, "Lenin, Leo Tolstoi, and Jesus Christ."

One of the travelers was quick to pick up on such an unusual observation. "Of these three great men, Lenin, Tolstoi, and Jesus Christ, which would you say is the greatest?" he inquired.

The guide quickly replied, "Lenin, of course."

Dr. Mecklenburg turned to the loyal guide and quietly asked, "Why do you say that Lenin was a greater character than Jesus Christ?"

The guide never hesitated as he responded, "People follow Lenin!"

Who will follow Jesus Christ? Who will put Him first in his life?

THE GREATEST NEED OF THE CHURCH

Text: II Cor. 8:5.
INTRODUCTION:

What is the greatest need of the church? Numbers? Organization? Faculties? Money?

Not more numbers — but better numbers.

Not better organization — but better devotion.

Not better buildings — but better lives.

Not more gifts of money — but more gifts of self.

Consecration in Hebrew literally means "to fill the hand."

PROPOSITION: II COR. 8:5 GIVES A CHALLENGING DEFINITION OF CONSECRATION.

  I. CONSECRATION IS AN OFFERING — "They gave."

  An offering made in answer to the love of Christ.

  This offering is to be made not in order to belong to Christ, but because we belong to Him. I Cor. 6:20.

 II. CONSECRATION IS A VOLUNTARY OFFERING — "Gave."

  There is one threshold God will not cross: human responsibility.

  "How oft would I, but ye would not" — Rev. 3:20.

III. CONSECRATION IS THE VOLUNTARY OFFERING OF SELF — "They gave themselves."

  It is *you* that God wants. Rom. 6:13.

  God does not want what you have until God can have you.

 IV. CONSECRATION IS THE VOLUNTARY OFFERING OF SELF TO GOD — "To the Lord."

  The question is not "Will I give myself to some specialized service?" but "Will I surrender my life to God, to let Him use it wherever He sees best?"

  V. CONSECRATION IS THE VOLUNTARY OFFERING OF SELF TO GOD AND MAN — "and to us."

  Service is the rent we owe mankind for the space we occupy on the earth.

  "God first — others second — I'm third."

 VI. CONSECRATION IS THE VOLUNTARY OFFERING OF SELF TO GOD AND MAN TO DO GOD'S WILL INSTEAD

OF OUR OWN — "According to the will of God."
How often the will of man conflicts with the will of God.
In such conflict, can we pray "Not my will, but thine be done?"
CONCLUSION:
Is the hand of God filled with you?
What would you do, where would you go, what would you be, if God had His perfect will in your life?

CONSECRATION

In the city of Rome, across the street from the Church of St. John Lateran, stands Pilate's Stairs. This is the stairway which Martin Luther was penitently climbing on hands and knees when he remembered that the just shall live by faith, and the Lutheran reformation was born.

It was a beautiful spring day, 1977. I stood near the foot of Pilate's Stairs and watched, rather idly I fear, as the faithful climbed the stairs on hands and knees, thinking to shorten their time in purgatory by such penance. Climb a step — finger their prayer beads — another step — another prayer.

Then suddenly I was jolted from my reverie by a gripping spectacle. A man who was terribly crippled in body carefully made his way to the foot of the stairs. Slowly and painfully he dragged his crippled body up a step and grasped his rosary. Slowly to the second step — and another prayer. A step — and a prayer — another step — another prayer — all the way to the top of that long stairway.

And, with tears stinging my eyes, I thought, "I have seen something; I have seen consecration; I have seen commitment!"

But that was not to be the end of the story. The cripple came once more to the foot of the stairs. Slowly and painfully he pulled that crippled body up a step and offered a prayer. Once more, and yet again, all the way to the top of Pilate's Stairs.

And we shake our heads and say, "Poor, ignorant heathen!" Perhaps, but if we who are members of the "New Testament Church" had more of the determination and devotion which moved the cripple to the top of Pilate's Stairs there is no power on earth or in hell that could stand in the way of the advancement of New Testament Christianity.

———————

It doesn't take much of a man to be a Christian —
but it takes every bit of him!

IF I WALK WHERE HE WALKED

Text: I John 2:6.

INTRODUCTION:

How many weary miles Jesus must have walked during His ministry.

How often we read the phrase "As He was walking."

". . . walking by the Sea of Galilee . . . walking in the temple .. . He entered and was passing through Jericho."

"He that saith he abideth in himn ought also to walk even as he walked."

PROPOSITION: WHERE I WILL WALK IF I WALK WHERE MY LORD WALKED.

I. IF I WALK WHERE HE WALKED I WILL WALK THE PATHWAY OF OBEDIENCE.

Matt. 3:13-17. It is a wonderful service to do that with which the Heavenly Father is well pleased.

II. IF I WALK WHERE HE WALKED I WILL WALK THE PATHWAY OF WORSHIP.

Luke 4:16; Matt. 14:23. Walking in the Lord's House and in the place of prayer.

III. IF I WALK WHERE HE WALKED I WILL WALK THE PATHWAY OF HOLINESS.

Matt. 4:1. The same power which enabled Him to overcome is available to me.

IV. IF I WALK WHERE HE WALKED I WILL WALK THE PATHWAY OF SERVICE.

1. Matt. 14:13-21. He walked where hungry folk were.
2. Mark 5:1-20. He walked where outcast folk were.
3. Matt. 14:22-33. He walked where discouraged folk were.
4. John 5:2-8. He walked where sick folk were.
5. John 11. He walked where sorrowing folk were.
6. John 4. He walked where sinful folk were.

V. IF I WALK WHERE HE WALKED I WILL WALK THE PATHWAY OF SACRIFICE.

John 19:17. This is the Man Who called, "If any man would come after me, let him deny himself, and take up his cross and follow me."

CONCLUSION:
>Have you learned to walk?
>If I walk where He walked I will walk with Him in life. Luke 24:15.
>If I walk where He walked I will walk with Him in glory. Rev. 3:4

OBEDIENCE

I said: "Let me walk in the fields."
He said: "No, walk in the town."
I said: "There are no flowers there."
He said: "No flowers, but a crown."

I said, "But the skies are black;
There is nothing there but noise and din."
And He wept as He sent me back —
"There is more," He said, "There is sin."

I said: "But the air is thick
And fogs are veiling the sun."
He answered: "Yet souls are sick
And souls in the dark undone!"

I said: "I shall miss the light,
And friends will miss me, they say."
He answered: "Choose tonight
If I am to miss you or they."

I pleaded for time to be given;
He said: "Is it hard to decide?
It will not seem so hard in heaven
To have followed the steps of your Guide."

I cast one look at the fields,
Then set my face to the town;
He said, "My child, do you yield?
Will you leave the flowers for the crown?"

IF I WALK WHERE HE WALKED

Then into His hand went mine;
  And into my heart came He;
And I walk in a light divine,
  The path I had feared to see.
                    —George MacDonald

WHO DO YOU THINK YOU ARE?

Text: Isa. 62:2.

INTRODUCTION:

    What's in a name? That which we call a rose
    by any other name would smell as sweet.

    But there is something in a name. Names are important. Names describe and designate. We love to hear our own name.

    God thinks names are important. Isa. 62:2.

PROPOSITION: GOD'S PEOPLE ARE DESCRIBED AND CHALLENGED BY DIVINELY GIVEN NAMES.

I. GOD'S PEOPLE ARE SAINTS. (This name appears 70 times in the N.T.)
   1. Saints are not sinless — Rom. 1:7.
   2. Saints are sanctified — Acts 20:32.
   3. Saints are trustees of a great heritage — Jude 3.
   4. Saints are partakers of a priceless inheritance — Col. 1:12.

II. GOD'S PEOPLE ARE DISCIPLES — Acts 6:1.
   1. Disciples obey their master — John 8:31.
   2. Disciples bear fruit — John 15:5.
   3. Disciples love one another — John 13:35.
   4. Disciples follow Christ — Luke 14:27.

III. GOD'S PEOPLE ARE BRETHREN — Acts 6:3.
   1. Brethren are related — Acts 22:13.
   2. Brethren are loving — I Pet. 2:17.
   3. Brethren are helpful — Acts 4:32-35.
   4. Brethren are forgiving — Eph. 4:32.

IV. GOD'S PEOPLE ARE CHRISTIANS — Acts 11:26.
   1. Christians declare their ownership — I Pet. 1:18-19.
   2. Christians glorify their owner — I Pet. 4:16
   3. Christians wear the one catholic (universal) name — Acts 26:28.
   4. God hasten the day that we will have done with our hyphenated distinctions.

CONCLUSION:

    Who do you think you are?

      With regard to character, a saint.

      With regard to occupation, a disciple.

With regard to relationship, a brother.
With regard to ownership, a Christian.
What a privilege and honor to become one whom God has
named.

THE LITTLE BEARS

Two dusky sons of the south served as guides to the bear hunters in
the swamps of South Carolina. First, there was Henry, 240-pound
Henry, big and strong, stripped to the waist, striding effortlessly all
day long as he directed the hunters. Then there was William, little,
scrawny, meek William. William was also a bear-hunting guide — all
110 pounds of him.

Little 110-pound William was a great admirer of 240-pound
Henry. One day 110-pound William fawned upon 240-pound Henry
and said, "Henry, if I was a great big strong man like you, you know
what I'd do? I'd go down dere in dat ol' swamp, and I'd find de big-
gest bear in dat swamp, and I'd jus' tear him to pieces with my bare
hands."

240-pound Henry looked with disdain on 110-pound William and
replied, "William, dey's still plenty ob little bears in dat swamp."

. . . and there is! I dare say there is one just about your size.
Whatever your position in life, and whatever your abilities, never con-
tent yourself with less than your best. Your best for God is wonderfully
important!

We can't all be captain; there must be crew. If you can't be the
captain, and must be a member of the crew, be mighty sure that you
are the very best little swab on the deck. . . . If you can't be the sun or
the moon, then just be a star in the heavens. . . . If you can't be a big
oak tree, then just be a shrub, but be the sturdiest little shrub on the
hillside. . . . Be the best of whatever you are!

ARE YOU —

FOOLISH enough to depend on Him for wisdom?
WEAK enough to be empowered with His strength?
BASE enough to have no honor but God's honor?
DESPISED enough to be kept in the dust at His feet?
NOTHING enough for God to be everything?

WRONG PLACES FOR SAINTS

Text: Gen. 3:9.

INTRODUCTION:

God created man, placed him in a perfect home, gave him dominion.

The creature rebelled against the Creator and lost his habitation.

God's question to His sinful creature is directed to us all: "Where art thou?"

PROPOSITION: MAY A LOOK AT GOD'S MISPLACED SAINTS AID US IN FINDING AND OCCUPYING OUR PLACE.

   I. ADAM IN THE BUSHES — Gen. 3:10.
   Sin always separates from God, but "you cannot hide from God" — Heb. 4:13. "Be sure your sins will find you out."

   II. ELIJAH IN A CAVE — I Kgs. 19:9-14.
   Elijah gave in to discouragement — verse 14.
   God's encouraging reply — verses 15-18.

   III. JONAH ON A SHIP — Jonah 1:1-3.
   Jonah had been given a commission which he tried to avoid.
   After Jonah's lesson he "arose and went," and a city was saved.

   IV. PETER AT A BONFIRE — Luke 22:55.
   When Peter got in the wrong crowd he denied Jesus.
   Peter came back. He became "the rock" on Pentecost.

   V. JUDAS IN THE SANHEDRIN — Matt. 26:14-16.
   Judas was treasurer of the band of disciples, but he was a thief.
   Following the anointing of Jesus with the costly ointment, he covenanted to sell his Lord for the price of a slave.

   VI. MARTHA IN THE KITCHEN — Luke 10:40.
   It was good to provide hospitality for Jesus; it was better to sit at His feet. Mary chose "the better part." If you have the hands of Martha, be sure you have the mind of Mary.

   VII. JOHN MARK IN JERUSALEM — Acts 13:13.
   Mark was chosen as a missionary, but returned to his home, leaving others to do the work the Lord had given him to do.
   "Be ye stedfast, unmovable, always abounding in the work of the Lord."

CONCLUSION:
   What results when saints are misplaced?
   1. Man is separated from God.
   2. God's work is hindered.
   3. Precious souls are lost for time and eternity.
      Are you a misplaced saint? If so, come back to God; He
      needs you.

THE LIGHT MUST BURN

"You'd be wise not to go up into the lighthouse tonight," one of the villagers warned the old lighthouse keeper as he prepared to make his way out to the light. "The way the foundation is breaking up, it just might not stand the storm."

"I know my duty, friend," came the old man's stern reply. "Forty years, and I've never missed a night. Storm or not, I must go. The light must burn."

All through the night he kept the light burning, even though the storm grew ever more violent. Each wave crashed against the foundation, sending a tremor through the aged structure. Finally in the early morning hours, before the first glimmerings of dawn, the foundation gave way, and the lighthouse slid into the foaming sea. Thus the old man perished, needlessly it seemed. But several weeks later the story took a different turn. Then it was learned that in the midst of the storm a naval vessel had passed within a few hundred yards of the dangerous reef marked by the lighthouse. The warning light had allowed the ship to pass in safety. And the captain of that ship was the old lighthouse keeper's son.

—John W. Wade

A blind man went about with a lantern on his arm. Someone asked him why he carried a lantern inasmuch as he was blind. He replied, "To keep other people from stumbling over me." That is something to think about.

—The Gospel Herald

WHOSE SIDE ARE YOU ON?

As the Yankees came marching into the South in the ebbing days of the Civil War, Granny grabbed a broom and ran into the road to meet the advancing army. Her daughter called out, "Granny, come back! What do you think you can do with that broom?"

"Well, at least I can show them whose side I'm on," came the resolute reply.

QUO VADIS?

Text: Phil. 3:13-14.

INTRODUCTION:

> The Church of God is a living organism. The church can not remain static; it is going to move, but which way? Quo Vadis?
>
> There is only one way for the Lord's people to go.
>
> Challenge of Exod. 14:15: "Speak unto the children of Israel, that they go forward."

PROPOSITION: PHIL. 3:13-14 REVEALS THE SECRET OF CHRISTIAN ADVANCEMENT.

I. ONE THING I DO.

> The secret of concentrated effort.
>
> The Christian does not have a multiplicity of tasks.
>
> To go forward seek first His kingdom and His righteousness.

II. FORGETTING THOSE THINGS WHICH ARE BEHIND.

> Did not mean forgetting in the sense of obliterating from the memory, but losing sight of the past as we catch the vision splendid for the future.

III. STRETCHING FORWARD TO THOSE WHICH ARE BEFORE.

> This implies effort ("stretching") and vision ("the things before").
>
> What do you see as you look to the future? The future is in the hand of the believer.
>
> The future is as bright as the promises of God.

IV. I PRESS ON.

> (Three of the biggest "little" words in the English language.)
>
> 1. "I" — one life: a splendid thing — with God.
> 2. "Press" — battle, conflict, struggle. The word for a time like this.
>   "Fight the good fight of the faith" — I Tim. 6:12.
> 3. "On" — the divine direction.
>   The difficult way: the hill-climbing way, but the way out.

CONCLUSION:

> The church is going — which way?
>
> The only ones who can answer are you who comprise the church.

The church will move in the divine direction when we learn to say, "But one thing I do, forgetting the things which are behind, and stretching forward to the things which are before, I press on toward the goal unto the prize of the high calling of God in Christ Jesus."

A CALL FOR VOLUNTEERS

It was during the early days of the Korean conflict and the fighting was fierce. A division of U.S. troops had withdrawn into the perimeter of safety. Their respite was short lived, for there came a call from the commanding general stating that the enemy had captured a near-by hill and that coming down the far side of the hill was a division of U.S. soldiers. The general added, "It is a dangerous mission, and I do not feel that I can order you to attack." The major who took the call quickly responded, "The hill will be taken."

The major assembled his troops and explained the situation: If they did nothing a division of soldiers would perish. The major continued, "I am not ordering you to attack, I am asking for volunteers." Drawing a line in the dust with the toe of his boot, the commander said, "Those who will follow me step across the line." The leader turned his back on his men and started toward the hill. At the foot of the hill he turned and looked back. The ranks were unbroken. Every soldier had stepped forward!

The battle was joined. The hill was taken. A division of soldiers was saved — and the major was one of the 70% of that regiment that did not return from the hill.

One day, many years ago, our Commander died on a hill. He does not command a following; He calls for volunteers. Will you be enlisted as a volunteer?

—as related by Chap. Col. Hal Martin

A call for loyal soldiers comes to one and all;
Soldiers for the conflict, will you heed the call!
Will you answer quickly, with a ready cheer,
Will you be enlisted as a volunteer?

QUO VADIS?

A volunteer for Jesus, A soldier true!
Others have enlisted, Why not you?
Jesus is the Captain, we will never fear;
Will you be enlisted as a volunteer?

GOOD STEWARDS

Text: I Pet. 4:10.
INTRODUCTION:
 "Stewardship" — a good word with a bad reputation.
 The custom of wealthy Jews to place a trusted servant over all affairs of the house. He was the "steward." Stewardship speaks of management, not ownership.
 Our faithfulness in stewardship is rooted in the vitality of our conversion.
 Peter outlines the Christian stewardship in I Pet. 4:7-11.
PROPOSITION: QUALIFICATIONS, RESPONSIBILITIES, AND PRIVILEGES OF THE CHRISTIAN STEWARD ARE FOUND IN THIS SCRIPTURE.

I. STEWARDS ARE TO BE OF SOUND MIND AND MEN OF PRAYER — v. 7.
 God wants His stewards to be good business men.
 Luke 16:1-11.

II. STEWARDSHIP IS TO BE RENDERED IN LOVE — v. 8.
 Service without love is no service at all.
 "Service is love in work clothes."

III. STEWARDS ARE TO HELP ONE ANOTHER — v. 9.
 Hospitality must not become a forgotten virtue.
 Gal. 6:10.

IV. WE ARE STEWARDS OF TALENT — v. 10.
 Every converted man is an endowed man.
 I Cor. 1:26-27. Your best for God is wonderfully important.

V. WE ARE STEWARDS OF A MESSAGE — v. 11a.
 Stewards are to be messenger boys, not authors.
 I Cor. 9:16-17.

VI. WE ARE STEWARDS OF A MINISTRY — v. 11b.
 Minister: "to act as a deacon, a servant."
 Not through our own strength, but of the strength which God supplieth.

VII. THE END OF OUR STEWARDSHIP — v. 11c.
 The crown of our stewardship is not to serve ourselves, nor to be recognized, nor to aid others, but to glorify God.
CONCLUSION:

Are we good stewards of the manifold grace of God?
God never called His stewards to be brilliant or popular or successful, but He did call them to be faithful. I Cor. 4:1-2.
There can be no proper stewardship without recognizing our owner and dedicating our lives to Him.

GIVE — AND IT SHALL BE GIVEN

It is the law of the Great Mathematician that His children never lost by sharing.

At the Wi-Ne-Ma Week of Missions, 1976, Jim Moon Kim shared the following splendid stewardship illustration.

A wealthy plantation owner had as his hobby the raising of thoroughbred horses. He was inordinately proud of his stock and wanted the very best for them. Since he was an elderly man, he felt that he should draw up a will in which he would provide for his horses, as well as make provision for his three sons.

When the old man died and his will was read it was found to contain the following stipulations: the oldest son was to receive one-half of the horses, the second son one-fourth of the horses, and the youngest son one-fifth of the horses. When the horses were counted they numbered nineteen head. What to do? No way could they carry out the stipulations of the will without killing the horses. Dilemma!

A wise neighbor found the answer: he gave the boys another horse, making a total of twenty. The oldest boy recieved one half: ten; the second son received one-fourth: five; the youngest son received one-fifth: four. This made a total of nineteen horses, so the donor took back his horse!

"Give, and it shall be given unto you" — Luke 6:38.

A man there was, some called him mad —
The more he gave away, the more he had.
—John Bunyan

Here lies a miser who lived for himself,
And cared for nothing but gathering wealth;
Now where he is, or how he fares,
Nobody knows and nobody cares.

A preacher was asked by one of his wealthiest members if he would get into heaven if he left all of his money to the church. Without pausing to debate the theological problems presented by the question, the minister quickly replied, "It's worth a try!"

THE KEY TO SUCCESS

Text: I Cor. 3:9.

INTRODUCTION:

The church at Corinth was a problem-filled church.

List some of their problems: division, apostasy, incest, improper observance of the Lord's Supper, spiritual gifts.

In spite of their problems, the church was successful.

Successful in that they purged the church, reached souls, grew numerically and spiritually.

Paul's rebuke and challenge to the church at Corinth: I Cor. 3:1-15.

PROPOSITION: LET US LEARN THE SECRET OF SUCCESS AS FOUND IN I COR. 3:9.

I. IF WE ARE TO SUCCEED WE MUST BE **WORKERS**.
  1. Work strengthens faith. It is not the workers who lose faith.
  2. Work renews spiritual life. Bodies grow strong through exercise.
  3. Work purifies the church. It is when professed Christians are at ease in Zion that the works of the flesh are manifest.

II. IF WE ARE TO SUCCEED WE MUST WORK **TOGETHER**.
  1. The work to be done demands it. John 17:20-21.
  2. We can do together what we can not do separately.
  3. Then it remains for us to find and occupy our place. Rom. 12:4-8.

III. IF WE ARE TO SUCCEED WE MUST WORK TOGETHER **WITH GOD**.
  1. Our Lord set the example.
     "My Father worketh until now, and I work" — John 5:17.
  2. God wants to be man's partner.
  3. The last promise the Son of God made to His people: "Lo, I am with you."
     He never broke a promise. Trust Him!

CONCLUSION:

Would you be successful in the Lord's work?
  1. Be a worker. Whatever your hand finds to do, do it with all your might.
  2. Work together, held within the bond of divine love.

3. Work together with God, for He has promised, "He will in no wise fail thee, neither will He in any wise forsake thee." . . . and your labor shall not go unrewarded.

A SHOW OF HANDS

She was just a frail young girl who had lost her mother, but she labored tirelessly to raise her little brothers and sisters until her own health broke. While in the hospital, with death approaching, she was visited by a deaconess from one of our churches. As they visited, the girl was lamenting that she had been able to do so little for Jesus.

The wise and compassionate deaconess replied, "Just show Jesus your hands, dear; just show Jesus your hands!"

Let's have a show of hands as we work together with God.

WHAT IS THAT IN THY HAND?

Shamgar had an ox-goad,
Rahab had a string,
Gideon had a trumpet,
David had a sling,
Samson had a jaw bone,
Moses had a rod,
Dorcas had a needle —
All were used for God.

No matter what others are doing, my friend,
Or what they are leaving undone,
God's counting on you to keep on with the job
'Til the very last battle is won.

He's counting on you to be faithful;
He's counting on you to be true.
Yes, others may work, or others may shirk,
But remember — God's counting on you.
—Author Unknown

I asked, "Why doesn't someone do something?"
Then I realized that I was someone.

A CURE FOR HEART TROUBLE

Text: John 14:1-6.

INTRODUCTION:

What would you do if you knew this was your last night on earth? Only those things you consider to be of utmost importance.

Jesus knew! In the fulness of that knowledge, He devoted time to prayer; He ate a farewell meal with His followers; He washed their feet; He spoke words of comfort.

It was a time of troubled hearts, and the Great Physician prescribed the cure: John 14:1-6.

PROPOSITION: JESUS' FORMULA WILL CURE TROUBLED HEARTS.

I. FAITH IN GOD. — "Believe in God." (Believe in God we must!)
   1. "The heavens declare the glory of God". . . . Psa. 19:1.
   2. "As the hart panteth after the water brooks". . . . Psa. 42:1.
   3. "He that hath seen me hath seen the Father". . . . John 14:9.

II. FAITH IN JESUS — "Believe also in me."
   1. The divine record causes us to believe in Him. John 20:30-31.
   2. Transformed lives cause us to believe in Him. II Cor. 5:17.
   3. Assurance in Christian hearts causes us to believe in Him. II Tim. 1:12.

III. THE MANY MANSIONS — "In my Father's house are many mansions."
   1. "If it were not so". . . . What we would expect from such a Christ.
   2. "I go to prepare". . . . A prepared place for a prepared people.
   3. "Many mansions". . . . There is room for all.

IV. HIS COMING AGAIN — "I will come again."
   1. The promise of One Who never told a lie.
   2. He is coming visibly and unexpectedly — Rev. 1:7; Matt. 24:42.

3. He is coming to receive His own — I Thess. 4:16-17.
V. THE PLAIN WAY — "I am the way."
  1. It is a narrow way — Matt. 7:13-14.
  2. It is a broad way — John 3:16.
  3. It is the only way that leads home — verse 6.
CONCLUSION:
  Do you have a troubled heart?
  Trust the Great Physician — He never lost a case!

FAIRER THAN DAY

One of our most effective missionaries in the orient is Yoon Kwon Chae. He ministers tirelessly. Exhausted, ill, and inadequate, he presses on. Day after day he teaches and preaches. He leads an effective institute to train native teachers and preachers. He oversees a large children's home. He and his wife have adopted several Korean children. His writings reflect an overflowing heart of love and compassion. Many of us have heard Chae relate the story of his conversion to Christ.

It was during the communist invasion of Korea, and Chae had gone to look for the body of his preacher father whom the communists had slain. There were many others on the same sorrowful mission that day. There were so many blackened corpses that Chae could not identify the body of his father. The bereaved ones about him were crying in hopelessness and despair. It was a scene of heartbreak.

But then, as the futile search continued, a grieving Christian looked up and lifted his voice in song: "There's a land that is fairer than day, and by faith we can see it afar; for the Father waits over the way, to prepare us a dwelling place there." Another voice joined in, others picked up the refrain, and soon a great chorus was swelling the song of assurance: "In the sweet by and by, we shall meet on that beautiful shore." Over and over again, they sang their song of hope and trust.

When the singing was ended every eye was dry and they were looking up with a new-found hope and faith. It was then and there that Yoon Kwon Chae gave himself to Christ and launched a life of dedicated Christian service.

A CURE FOR HEART TROUBLE

One little hour of watching with the Master,
    Eternal years to walk with Him in white,
One little hour to bravely meet disaster,
    Eternal years to reign with Him in light,
One little hour for weary toils and trials,
    Eternal years for calm and peaceful rest,
One little hour for patient self-denials,
    Eternal years for life, where life is blest.

BIBLE VERSES THAT BOTHER ME

Text: II Pet. 3:15-16.

INTRODUCTION:

Some are bothered by Gen. 4:16-17 — Where did Cain get his wife?

Some are bothered by Matt. 1:18 — How was the virgin birth possible?

Some are bothered by I Cor. 15:29 — What does "baptism for the dead" mean?

Mark Twain: "Most people are bothered by those passages in Scripture which they do not understand, but as for me, I always noticed that the passages in Scripture which trouble me are those which I do understand."

PROPOSITION. BIBLE VERSES THAT BOTHER ME ARE THOSE I UNDERSTAND, BUT DO NOT ALWAYS HEED.

I. Heb. 12:14. SANCTIFICATION WITHOUT WHICH NO MAN SHALL SEE THE LORD.
   1. "Sanctify" means to set aside for a holy purpose, or to make holy.
   2. Bothers me, for without holy life I can not see God in this world or that to come. Matt. 5:8.

II. John 13:34-35. A NEW COMMANDMENT I GIVE UNTO YOU, THAT YE LOVE ONE ANOTHER.
   1. By this men know we are His disciples.
   2. Bothers me, for without love for my brother I do not have eternal life. I John 3:14-15.

III. Ezek. 3:16-21. I HAVE MADE THEE A WATCHMAN.
   1. The watchman is to warn the people. Ezek. 33:1-6.
   2. Bothers me, for if I do not warn I am guilty of my brother's blood.

IV. Dan. 12:3. THEY THAT TURN MANY TO RIGHTEOUSNESS. . . .
   1. His disciples are to witness that souls might be saved. Matt. 28:19.
   2. Bothers me, for unless I turn men to righteousness souls are lost and I shall lose my reward.

V. Matt. 25:31-46. INASMUCH AS YE DID IT UNTO ONE OF

THESE.
1. His disciples are to serve their fellowman. John 13:15.
2. Bothers me, for if I do not serve my fellowman the love of God does not abide in me. I John 3:17.

CONCLUSION:
The Bible verses that bother me are those which pertain to living, loving, proclaiming, winning, and serving.
Let us be bothered enough to obey when the Master speaks.

GOD, THOU HAST LIED

Once upon a time a very devout monk was praying in the temple when an angel appeared to him and said, "Go into the desert and God will speak to you there." So the monk got up and started out into the desert. As he journeyed he came upon a villager who said, "Kind monk, please help us build a wall so that the village may be saved from the flood." But the monk said, "I cannot, I must go into the desert, for God has promised to speak to me there." And he went on.

Farther on he met a man who was sitting on a rock, and the man said, "Kind monk, please stay with me tonight. I have just lost my wife and son and I do not want to stay alone." But the monk said, "I cannot, I must go into the desert, for God has promised to speak to me there." And he went on.

Farther on he met a young man who said, "Kind monk, teach me about Jesus so that I might be saved." But the monk said, "I cannot, I must go into the desert, for God has promised to speak to me there." And he went on.

Several years went by and the monk who was growing impatient said, "God, Thou hast lied to me. Thou hast promised to speak to me and have not."

And God answered him saying, "Three times I spoke to you and you did not hear. I spoke to you through the villager, I spoke to you through the man who lost his wife and son, and I spoke to you through the young man. You were so busy thinking of yourself that you did not hear me."

"Inasmuch as ye did it unto one of these my brethren, even these least,

97

ye did it unto me." Matt. 25:40.

WHAT IT COSTS TO BE FAITHFUL

It cost Abraham the yielding up of his only son.
It cost Esther the risk of her life.
It cost Daniel to be cast into the lion's den.
It cost Shadrach, Meshach, and Abednego being put
    into the fiery furnace.
It cost Stephen death by stoning.
It cost Peter a martyr's death.
It cost Jesus His life on the cross.

What is it costing you?

BINDING THE HANDS OF JESUS

Text: Matt. 27:1-2.
INTRODUCTION:

See the hands of Jesus:

1. They were strong hands. The toil-scarred hands of the carpenter.
   The hands that cleansed the temple and which were extended to the sinking Peter were strong hands.
2. They were tender hands. They touched sightless eyes; they were laid upon the leper; they took the hand of the daughter of Jairus; they gave the sop to Judas.
3. They were uplifted hands. He lifted up His hands in blessing. Little children were brought that He might lay His hands on them.
4. They were folded hands. Clasped often in prayer.
5. They were finally bound by those He sought to bless.

PROPOSITION: HOW WE ARE GUILTY OF BINDING THE HANDS OF JESUS.

   I. BY REJECTING HIS INVITATION.
      1. He will not force Himself upon us. Matt. 23:37.
      2. We can loose these bonds when we open the door. Rev. 3:20.
  II. BY DIVIDING HIS BODY.
      1. He prayed that His disciples might be one, that the world might believe. John 17:20-21.
      2. We can loose these bonds when we love one another. John 13:34-35.
 III. BY UNSANCTIFIED LIVES.
      1. He prayed for the sanctification of His disciples. John 17:17.
      2. We can loose these bonds when our lives are holy. Acts 4:13.
  IV. BY REFUSING TO SERVE.
      1. He set the example for our ministry. Matt. 4:23.
      2. We can loose these bonds when we serve our fellowman. Matt. 25:40.

CONCLUSION:

The nail-scarred hands of the Christ are outstretched in invitation.

See His hands — Free His hands — Be His hands.

> Place your hand in the nail-scarred hand,
> Place your hand in the nail-scarred hand;
> He will keep to the end, He's your dearest Friend,
> Place your hand in the nail-scarred hand.

THE WORLD'S BIBLE

A Chinese woman had just learned to read. "Lord," she prayed, "we are going home to many who cannot read. Make us living Bibles, so that those who cannot read the Book, can read it in us."

Christ has no hands but our hands to do His work today,
He has no feet but our feet to lead men in the way,
He has no tongue but our tongues to tell men how He died,
He has no help but our help to bring them to His side.

We are the only Bible the careless world will read,
We are the sinner's gospel, we are the scoffer's creed,
We are the Lord's last message, given in deed and word.
What if the type is crooked? What if the print is blurred?

What if our hands are busy with other work than His?
What if our feet are walking where sin's allurement is?
What if our tongues are speaking of things His lips would spurn?
How can we hope to help Him and hasten His return?

—Annie Johnson Flint

It was the close of World War II. Ruin and devastation abounded on every hand. Some thoughtful G.I.'s, awaiting their turn to transfer to the States, offered to help rebuild a ruined city. All help was refused until the mayor offered to let them restore the statue of Christ in the town square. The soldiers went to work and recovered all of the statue but the hands. When the statue was unveiled it was discovered that the builders had placed this inscription upon the handless statue, "I have no hands — won't you please loan me yours?"

THE FESTAL DAYS

NEW THINGS FOR THE NEW YEAR

Text: II Cor. 5:17.

INTRODUCTION:

Louise Tarkington expressed the longing of many hearts as she wrote, "I wish there were some beautiful place called the Land of Beginning Again."

There is such a place. There is but one way to find it:

Jesus to Nicodemus, "Except one be born anew . . ." John 3:1-5.

Saul of Tarsus became the new man, Paul the apostle.

All things become new in Christ. II Cor. 5:17.

PROPOSITION: AS YOU BEGIN A NEW YEAR, SEE THE NEW THINGS AVAILABLE THROUGH CHRIST.

 I. A NEW BODY.

A new concept of the house in which we live. I Cor. 6:20.

A new heart for a new love. A new head to think new thoughts. New lips to speak a new message. New eyes to see new things. New hands to do a new work. New feet to walk a new way.

 II. A NEW WAY.

The way foretold by the prophet — Isa. 35:8.

The new and living way — Heb. 10:20.

The only way — John 14:6.

 III. A NEW NAME.

Isa. 62:2; Rev. 2:17; I Pet. 4:16.

The name above every name. A sufficient name.

 IV. A NEW COMMANDMENT.

John 13:34; Matt. 22:37-40.

The new creature has no room for hate.

 V. A NEW SONG.

Psa. 40:1-3. The deeper the pit, the sweeter the song.

From the heart of the new creature flows a melody sweeter than song.

 VI. A NEW HOME.

II Pet. 3:13; Rev. 21:1-4.

The home toward which the new creature journeys: "a house

105

not made with hands, eternal, in the heavens." II Cor. 5:1.
CONCLUSION:
    This could be your finest year. Begin it with God.
    Be a new man — walking a new way — wearing a new name —
      obeying a new commandment —singing a new song — tra-
      veling to a new home.
    The way of the cross leads home.

LAND OF BEGINNING AGAIN

I wish that there were some wonderful place
Called the Land of Beginning Again,
Where all our mistakes and all our heartaches
And all our poor selfish grief
Could be dropped like a shabby old coat at the door
And never put on again.

I wish we could come on it all unawares,
Like the hunter who finds a lost trail,
And I wish that the one to whom our blindness had done
The greatest injustice of all
Could be at the gates, like an old friend that waits
For the comrade he's gladdest to hail.

We would all find the things we intended to do,
But forgot, and remembered too late,
Like praises unspoken, little promises broken,
And all the thousand and one
Little duties neglected that might have perfected
The day for one less fortunate.

It wouldn't be possible not to be kind
In the Land of Beginning Again.
The ones we misjudge, and the ones whom we grudged
Their moments of victory here,
Would find in the grasp of our loving handclasp
More than penitent lips could explain.

For what had been hardest we'd know had been best,
And what had seemed loss would be gain;
For there is not a sting that will not wing
When we've faced it and laughed it away —
And I think that the laughter is most what we're after,
In the Land of Beginning again.
                                    —Louise Tarkington

"Behold, I make all things new." Rev. 21:5.

NEW YEARS RESOLUTIONS

Text: Luke 16:4.

INTRODUCTION:

> At the year's end each receives a gift: a book with 365 blank pages.
>
> In this book you will be writing, day by day.
>
> How will your book look at the end of the year? This may be partially dependent upon resolutions you make as you begin the new year.
>
> It is human nature to make resolutions. Many Bible characters made resolutions.

PROPOSITION: LET US LEARN FROM RESOLUTIONS MADE BY BIBLE CHARACTERS.

I. A TRUSTED DISCIPLE — Matt. 26:15.

Judas' resolution: "I am resolved to get what I can, even though it costs the life of my Master."

He kept his resolution. He received his reward. In remorse, he committed suicide.

II. THE BIG FISHERMAN — Matt. 26:33.

Peter's resolution: "I will remain true, regardless the cost."

A few hours later Peter denied his Lord, but Peter came back.

III. A CERTAIN MAN — Luke 9:57.

His resolution: "I am resolved to follow Jesus."

We are not told how he kept his resolution. We assume that he failed the test — Luke 9:58.

IV. A POOR OLD RICH FARMER — Luke 12:16-21.

The farmer's resolution: "I am resolved to gain wealth, although I exclude God and man."

He kept his resolution. That night he lost his soul.

V. A GOVERNOR OF JUDAEA — Luke 23:16.

Pilate's resolution: "I will chastise him, and release him."

He did not keep his resolution. He yielded to mob pressure and the blood of the sinless Son of God was on his hands.

VI. A WAYWARD BOY — Luke 15:18.

The prodigal's resolution: "I will arise and go to my father."

He kept his resolution. He arose and came. He came all the
way. He was received by a loving, forgiving father.
CONCLUSION:
You have been given a new book. How will it look at the year's
end?
RESOLVE to go through the year with God.
He will give you a new start. Jer. 31:34; Isa. 1:18.
He will help you to have a book of which you need not be
ashamed.

THE GATE OF THE YEAR

I said to the man who stood at the Gate of the Year,
"Give me a light that I may tread safely into the unknown."
And he replied, "Go out into the darkness, and put your hand into the
hand of God.
That shall be to you better than light, and safer than a known way."
So I went forth, and finding the hand of God, trod gladly into the
night.
And He led me toward the hills and the breaking of day in the lone
East. . . .
The stretch of years which winds ahead, so dim in our imperfect
vision,
Are clear to God.
Our fears are premature;
In Him all time hath full provision."

—Muriel Haskins

NEW YEAR'S WISH

May you have —

ENOUGH . . . happiness to keep you sweet;
ENOUGH . . . trials to keep you strong;
ENOUGH . . . sorrow to keep you human;
ENOUGH . . . hope to make your heart sing;

ENOUGH . . . labor to keep you from rust;
ENOUGH . . . leisure to make you broad;
ENOUGH . . . religion to make you value the best;
ENOUGH . . . of the love of Christ in your soul
to make you glad to serve.

"Next year, when you are going to do better, is here."

A NEW CHURCH FOR THE NEW YEAR

Text: Josh. 3:4.

INTRODUCTION:

General Joshua was always God's man. He was appointed to lead God's people into the Land of Promise.

Joshua's instructions as they stood at the border of their new land: (Josh. 3) "Ye have not passed this way heretofore."

We stand today at the border of a new land: the new year.

What will we cause the church to be in this new year?

PROPOSITION: ROMANS 12 DEPICTS THE IDEAL CHURCH FOR THE NEW YEAR.

  I. A SACRIFICING CHURCH — v. 1.

Our bodies are to be presented because of the mercies of God.

This is our spiritual, or **reasonable** service.

 II. A TRANSFORMED CHURCH — v. 2.

The Christian life is the "different" life: transformed, not conformed.

This is the good and acceptable and perfect will of God.

III. A FUNCTIONING CHURCH — vs. 3-8.

A service to be rendered humbly — v. 3.

Do what we can — give what we have — vs. 4-8.

 IV. A LOVING CHURCH — vs. 9-10.

A genuine love (without hypocrisy) — v. 9.

A love that prefers one another — v. 10.

  V. A SERVING CHURCH — vs. 11-15.

Not slothful in this service: fervent, rejoicing, patient, undergirded with prayer.

Identifying with your fellowman — v. 15.

 VI. A UNITED CHURCH — vs. 16-19.

A united church is a happy and a winning church.

There is but one adequate bond: love.

VII. AN OVERCOMING CHURCH — vs. 20-21.

Overcoming enemies — v. 20. The best way to get rid of an enemy is to make him your friend.

Overcoming evil — v. 21. "Good" is the higher power.

111

CONCLUSION:
>We stand today on the border of a new year.
>The church of the New Year will be what you make it.
>If sacrificing, transformed, functioning, loving, serving, united, and overcoming, we will spend this year in the "Promised Land."

GETTING STARTED RIGHT

There is a story told of a four-year-old who had great difficulty persuading the button holes and buttons to come out even on his sweater. Again and again he would find himself at the top with an extra button and no buttonhole.

Then one day he made a great discovery! He found that if he started out right at the bottom that he would come out alright at the top. His problem was that of getting started right by getting the first button in the first button hole.

How often we find ourselves in this very situation as we begin a new year. We suddenly realize, as this young boy, that if we don't begin to make certain adjustments at the beginning of the new year, that our life will come out all wrong. Let us begin by putting God first in all things as we approach this new year. Remember what Jesus said: "Seek ye first the kingdom of God and His righteousness, and all these things shall be added unto you."

WISHES FOR THE NEW YEAR

BLESSINGS in abundance,
STRENGTH for every way,
COURAGE for each trial,
GLADNESS for each day.

FAITH in heaven's guidance,
HOPE that's firm and true,
May the Lord, our Saviour,
Give these gifts to you!

112

ASKING THE DAYS THAT ARE PASSED

Text: Deut. 4:32.

INTRODUCTION:

>Moses had led the people of God from the Land of Bondage to the Land of Promise.

>Before Israel crossed Jordan Moses recounts the story of wandering and the giving of the law.

>In our text Moses challenges Israel to learn from past experience: "Ask now of the days that are past. . . ."

>As we stand at the border of a new land, the new year, may we have learned from the days that are past.

PROPOSITION: WHAT WE SHOULD HAVE LEARNED FROM THE DAYS THAT ARE PAST.

I. HAVE WE LEARNED THAT WE CAN DO TOGETHER WHAT WE CAN'T DO SEPARATELY?
1. Jesus knew this secret — John 17:20-21.
2. Paul discovered this secret — I Cor. 3:9.
3. The early church utilized this secret — Acts 4:32-35.

II. HAVE WE LEARNED THAT OUR BEST FOR GOD IS WONDERFULLY IMPORTANT?
1. He expects us to use what we have — Matt. 25:14-30.
2. He chose the weak things to glorify Him — I Cor. 1:26-31.
3. A boy gave his lunch. A widow gave all she had. The disciples "little" became much when given to Him.

III. HAVE WE LEARNED THAT FIRST THINGS OUGHT COME FIRST?
1. Jesus outlined priorities for His people in Matt. 6:33.
2. His Kingdom ought come first, but many are majoring in minors.
3. What will you put **first** in this new year?

IV. HAVE WE LEARNED THE JOY OF BEING AN OVERCOMER?
1. Paul became a victor in the conflict — Rom. 7:24-25.
2. John points the way to becoming an overcomer — I John 4:4.

113

3. We can become overcomers through faith — I John 5:4.
CONCLUSION

New Years we stand on a mountain top and view the Promised
Land.

May we ask of the days that are past, that the lessons learned
may guide us to victory in the Land of Promise.

GOD LEADS INTO THE PROMISED LAND

"When ye see that ark of the covenant of Jehovah your God, and
the priests and the Levites bearing it, then ye shall remove from your
place, and go after it. Yet there shall be a space between you and it,
about two thousand cubits by measure, come not near unto it, that ye
may know the way by which ye must go; for ye have not passed this
way heretofore."

—Joshua 3:3-4

GO ON

A tired old doctor died today,
    and a baby boy was born —
A little new soul that was pink and frail,
    and a soul that was gray and worn.
And — halfway here and halfway there
On a white, high hill of shining air —
They met and passed and paused to speak
    in the flushed and hearty dawn.

The man looked down at the soft, small thing,
    with wise and weary eyes;
And the little chap stared back at him,
    with startled, scared surmise,
And then he shook his downy head —
"I think I won't be born," he said;
"You are too gray and sad!" And he shrank
    from the the pathway down the skies.

114

But the tired old doctor roused once more
   at the battle-cry of birth,
And there was memory in his look,
   of grief and toil and mirth.
"Go on!" he said, "It's good — and bad:
It's hard! Go on! It's ours, my lad."
And he stood and urged him out of sight,
   down to the waiting earth.

EASTER VERBS

Text: Matt. 28:5-7.

INTRODUCTION:

> Earth's saddest day and earth's gladdest day just three days apart.

> Friday was a sad day. The Nazarene had been denied, betrayed, arrested, abused, and crucified.

> Women who had loved Him prepared spices to anoint His dead body.

> Those who were last at the cross were first at the tomb. Here they saw heavenly messengers and heard the heavenly message (text)

PROPOSITION: THE MESSAGE OF EASTER IS FOUND IN THESE RESURRECTION VERBS: FEAR NOT — COME SEE — GO TELL.

  I. FEAR NOT.

    1. The Christian faith is filled with "fear nots." 365 in the Bible: one for every day in the year.

    2. When Jesus said "Fear not:" Matt. 14:27; Luke 8:50; 12:32; Rev. 1:17; 2:10.

    3. With the risen Christ we face life fearlessly. I Pet. 3:14; I John 4:18. Song: "Because He lives all fear is gone."

  II. COME SEE.

    1. It is a tomb: a place of darkness and death.

    2. It is a new tomb — a rich man's tomb — a borrowed tomb. It is in a garden, a place of life and beauty.

    3. It is empty. The infidel Schenkel asserted, "It is an indisputable fact that in the early morning of the first day of the week following the crucifixion, the grave was found empty."

  III. GO TELL.

    1. Tell what? "He is risen." Not "He has risen." The tense is everything!

    2. Tell who? "His disciples." Mark adds "and Peter." What an encouragement to those who have denied Him.

3. The response to the commission: "They departed
quickly . . . with fear and great joy."
CONCLUSION:
This is the meaning and the message of Easter: "Fear not —
Come see — Go tell."
What difference has Easter made to you?
If you will go forth with your hand placed firmly in the nail-
scarred hand, your feet on the King's high road that leads
heavenward, your heart opened to the living Christ, and
your mouth opened to share the triumphant story — then
you have found the message of Easter.

EASTER LILIES

Our sanctuary is graced this morning by these creamy white Easter
lilies. How beautiful and how fragrant they are! But they were not
always thus. A few short weeks ago this lily was a dry, dirty bulb. To
the outward eye it was dead. Skilled hands buried it in mother earth
but, as time went by, something glorious happened. There came a
resurrection! Above the grave appeared a stalk of green, and it grew,
and it matured, and it put forth the blossoms which adorn our place of
worship this morning. It is the law of the Creator that life must follow
death.

"No," rasped old Jonathan, "I don't agree
With any resurrection, neither mind,
Body nor Spirit, beast nor humankind;
That takes belief too credulous for me.
I'm a blunt man, who never put much stock
In theories a person can't explain
All right and clear — it goes against the grain
To listen to this 'faith and wonders' talk."

He turned with one last sniff and dropped a brown
Seed pellet in the loosely furrowed drill —
Another and another — squatted down

117

To rearrange the earth with loving skill.
"By June," he bragged, "I'll have nasturtiums here
Bigger'n the ones you raved about last year."
                              —Florence Burrill Jacobs

WHO MOVED THE STONE?

Text: Matt. 28:1-2.

INTRODUCTION:

The facts:

1. A baby named Jesus was born.
2. He grew to manhood in Palestine.
3. For 3½ years He went about doing good.
4. He was betrayed, condemned, crucified and buried. A great stone sealed His tomb.
5. On the third day the tomb was found empty. WHO MOVED THE STONE?

PROPOSITION: THE DIVINELY MOVED STONE IS THE BASIS OF EASTER.

  I. THE SKEPTIC'S ANSWER.

    1. His friends moved the stone.
    Impossible! The tomb was sealed with the Roman seal and guarded by Roman soldiers.
    2. His enemies moved the stone.
    For what purpose? They did not desire a "resurrection story."
    3. The human Jesus moved the stone (the "swoon theory.")
    One who had suffered the rigors of the crucifixion could have convinced no one that He was conqueror of death.

  II. THE SCRIPTURAL ANSWER.

    1. An angel rolled away the stone. Matt. 28:2.
    2. The mark of deity is written all over the resurrection story. Man could not have fabricated such a story. It is written as it is because that is the way it happened.
    3. The resurrection is the counterpart of the virgin birth. It is just what you would expect from such a God.

  III. THE SIGNIFICANCE OF THE EMPTY TOMB.

    1. Jesus is declared to be the Son of God. Rom. 1:4.
    2. Those who believe in Him are justified. Rom. 4:25.
    3. Believers shall live eternally with the risen Lord. II Cor. 5:1.

CONCLUSION:

What does it mean to you that God moved the stone?
Easter is the announcement of a fact . . . the pronouncement
of a purpose . . . the appropriation of a power.

Christ Jesus lay in death's strong bands,
    For our offenses given;
But now at God's right hand He stands,
    And offers life from Heaven.

THERE'S NOTHING IN THERE

The highlight of touring the Holy Land is experienced at the
Garden Tomb. Just a short distance north of the city wall of Old
Jerusalem we come to "Skull Hill." This is Gordon's Calvary, and
may well be the "green hill far away" on which our Lord was
crucified.

The enclosed garden nearby is a refuge of beauty and peace. The
gravel pathways wind under hovering tree and beside beautiful flowers
and well-kept shrubbery. It is but a short distance from Calvary to the
tomb. The tomb is hewn out of soft white limestone. Before the tomb
is a channel where the "great stone" may well have been rolled in
place. And the tomb is empty.

A society matron, who was touring the Holy Land as something of
a status symbol, was invited to enter the tomb. Somewhat reluctantly
she entered, looked about for a moment, and then said in disgust,
"Why, there's nothing in there!"

What a beautiful contrast as one of the fine young ladies of our
tour group bowed her head and reverently entered the tomb. She
emerged with face aglow and, with arms lifted high above her head,
she exulted, "He isn't there! Praise God, He isn't there!"

I serve a risen Saviour, He's in the world today;
I know that He is living, whatever men may say;
I see His hand of mercy, I hear His voice of cheer,
And just the time I need Him He's always near.

The stone wasn't moved to permit Jesus to arise;
It was moved to permit disciples to enter and believe.

ON THE EMMAUS WAY

Text: Luke 24:13.

INTRODUCTION:

Relate last events in the life of Christ: crucifixion, burial, the unbelievable story which the women had brought to the disciples.

Two disciples were traveling from Jerusalem to Emmaus on resurrection day. (A village about 7 miles west of Jerusalem.)

One of them is named, the other is not. The other disciple may be you.

PROPOSITION: LET US LEARN THE LESSONS OF THE EMMAUS ROAD. Luke 24:13-35.

I. ON THE EMMAUS WAY THEY COMMUNED WITH EACH OTHER — v. 14.

1. The topic of their conversation: "The things which had happened."

2. We do well to commune with each other concerning Jesus.

II. ON THE EMMAUS WAY JESUS DREW NEAR AND WENT WITH THEM — v. 15.

1. What a blessed walk when the Master walks with us.

2. They failed to recognize Him. "Their eyes were holden."

III. ON THE EMMAUS WAY JESUS SPOKE — v. 17.

1. "And they stood still, looking sad," and well they might, for their hopes lay buried in the garden of Joseph of Arimathea.

2. He interpreted to them . . . the things concerning himself.

IV. ON THE EMMAUS WAY THEY INVITED HIM IN — vs. 28-29.

1. "He made as though he would go further." How nearly they missed the blessing.

2. He will never be the intruder. You must invite Him in.

V. ON THE EMMAUS WAY THEIR EYES WERE OPENED — vs. 30-31.

1. He was made known in the breaking of bread.

2. They saw again those familiar hands (relate what those

hands had done. . . .) now breaking the bread.
VI. ON THE EMMAUS WAY THERE WERE BURNING
HEARTS AND SWIFT FEET — vs. 32-35.
1. The world is dying for want of men with hot hearts.
2. Their message: "The Lord is risen indeed." Not "the Lord
has risen." The message of Easter can not be written in the
past tense.
COCLUSION:
Will you walk with Him on the Emmaus way?
Will you invite Him in?
Will you discover the message of Easter?
Will you have burning hearts and swift feet, and tell the world
that He is not a dead king, but a living Saviour?

GRAVE NOT A TERMINUS

A little lad was gazing intently at the picture in the art store window: the store was displaying a notable picture of the crucifixion. A
gentleman approached, stopped, and looked. The boy, seeing his in-
terest, said: "That's Jesus." The man made no reply, and the lad continued: "Them's Roman soldiers." And, after a moment: "They
killed Him."

"Where did you learn that?" asked the man.

"In the Mission Sunday-school," was the reply.

The man turned and walked thoughtfully away. He had not gone
far when he heard a youthful voice calling: "Say mister," and quickly
the little street lad caught up with him. "Say, Mister," he repeated, "I
wanted to tell you that He rose again."

That message, which was nearly forgotten by the boy, is the
message which has been coming down through the ages. It is the resurrection message — the story of the eternal triumph of life over death,
the promise and pledge of man's immortality.

The grave to Him was not a terminus!

This is the day of glad tidings! Go quickly, and tell the message!
"He is risen!" Hallelujah! Christ is risen! Hades could not hold Him!
Corruption could not devour Him! "I am He that liveth and was

dead; and behold, I am alive forevermore, Amen; and have the keys
of death and Hades.'' Blessed be God! Jesus lives to die no more! Go
quickly, and tell everyone the glad news!

> And I think the Shining Ones marvel much
> As they gaze from the world above,
> To see how slowly we spread the news
> Of that sacrifice of love.

THREE THOUSAND PROOFS
OF THE RESURRECTION

Text: Acts 2:41

INTRODUCTION:

Christianity stands or falls with the resurrection of Jesus.

Faith in the resurrection is essential to salvation — Rom. 10:9.

There is no more firmly established fact in history than the resurrection of Jesus Christ. List evidences of the resurrection.

No unprejudiced court in the world, upon hearing testimony of such witnesses, would leave Him in the tomb.

50 days after the resurrection there were 3,000 authentic proofs.

PROPOSITION: MAY OUR LIVES BE PROOFS OF THE RESURRECTION.

I. 3,000 HEARD THE MESSAGE — v. 22.
1. They heard of the death, burial, and resurrection of the Messiah.
2. They heard that God had made Him Lord and Christ — v. 36.

II. 3,000 BELIEVED THE MESSAGE — v. 37.
1. They believed Jesus was the Messiah, crucified and risen.
2. They believed that they were guilty and needed salvation.

III. 3,000 DESIRED TO BE SAVED — v. 37.
1. They earnestly inquired, "What shall we do?"
2. The inspired answer: "Repent, and be baptized."

IV. 3,000 OBEYED THE LORD'S COMMAND — v. 41.
1. They received his word. They repented and were baptized.
2. They experienced the fulfillment of the promise: remission of sins and gift of the Holy Spirit.
3. If you will obey the same commands, you will experience the same results and will be added to Christ's church.

V. 3,000 CONTINUED STEDFASTLY — v. 42.
1. Their conversion was not an "end," but a beginning.
2. Converts must continue in these acts of worship.

CONCLUSION:

The resurrected life is the greatest proof of the resurrection.
"If then ye were raised together with Christ, seek the things that
   are above, where Christ is, seated at the right hand of God."
   — Col. 3:1.
How far have you gone with the 3,000?
You have heard. You believe. Will you obey?

WERE YOU THERE?

The beautifully familiar negro spiritual, in haunting refrain, asks
the question, "Were you there when they crucified my Lord?"

Were you there when they crucified my Lord?
Were you there when they crucified my Lord?
Oh sometimes it causes me to tremble, tremble, tremble.
Were you there when they crucified my Lord?

I was there when Jesus died, for on the cross He took my place and
identified with me and I with Him. I was with Him on that day when I
made my decision to be crucified with Christ and die to the old life
that I might find new life in Him.
   "Were you there when they laid Him in the tomb?" I was, when as
just a lad, I was buried with Him in the cold waters of Elk Creek, in
Douglas County, Oregon. I shall always remember and cherish that
day of complete and joyful surrender.
   "Were you there when He rose up from the tomb?" I was there ,
and I was with Him when I was "raised to walk in newness of life,"
and became a new creature in Him.
   How wonderful that by obeying His commands we may re-enact
the facts of the gospel: the death, burial, and resurrection of our
Lord. It is all there in Rom. 6:1-4: Christ died, and we "died to sin."
Christ was buried, and we were "buried with him through baptism."
Christ was raised, and we also "walk in newness of life."

125

BIBLE MOTHERS

Text: John 19:27.

INTRODUCTION:

A day set aside to honor mothers. Rightly so, for we are deeply indebted to the mothers of the world. Mother gave us life, love, counsel. Sacrificed for our well being.

Mothers are given a place of prominence in the Scripture; the word "mother" appears more than 300 times on its pages.

A time like this demands good mothers.

PROPOSITION: MOTHERS OF THE BIBLE GIVE US IDEALS FOR MOTHERHOOD.

I. JOCHEBED, THE COURAGEOUS MOTHER — Exo. 2.
   1. She had courage to hide her child from a jealous king.
   2. She was her child's nurse and teacher, and he became leader and law-giver for God's people.

II. HANNAH, THE PRAYING MOTHER — I Sam. 1.
   1. She looked upon motherhood as a privilege. She prayed for a child.
   2. All Israel knew that the child would be a prophet — I Sam. 3:20.

III. MARY, THE SUBMISSIVE MOTHER — Luke 1:38.
   1. The Israelitish maiden, without hesitation, responded, "Be it done unto me according to thy word."
   2. She endured the piercing of the sword — Luke 2:35.

IV. EUNICE, THE TEACHING MOTHER — II Tim. 1:5.
   1. She taught her child the sacred writings — II Tim. 3:15.
   2. "If the women of this country, the mothers, would teach the lessons of God as prescribed in His Book to their children, we could dispense with more than half of our jails." —Judge Fasset

V. THE CANAANITISH WOMAN, THE PERSISTENT MOTHER — Matt. 15:21-28.
   1. She faced many obstacles: she was a woman, a foreigner, disciples interfered, Jesus' apparent rudeness.
   2. She persisted in bringing her child to Jesus, and the story of

her faith and persistence still stand as a challenge to us.
CONCLUSION:
May mothers of the Bible be an inspiration to mothers of our day.
Recapitulation. . . .
Will you be this kind of mother?

CHRIST IN MOTHER'S EYES

I've seen the highest mountains
That this world has to show;
I've seen the longest rivers
That to the ocean flow.
But the thing I hold in memory —
That never, never dies,
Is the one thing long remembered —
I saw Christ in Mother's eyes.

I've known worldly sorrows
That death alone can bring,
Of deep heart-felt contrition,
That comes to one who sins,
But in my heart lies buried
And will till memory dies,
Is the picture God emplanted —
I saw Christ in Mother's eyes.

My heart has oft been hardened
To the hurts that others give;
I've often felt like giving up —
I didn't want to live.
But new hope, ever born anew,
Has caused my hopes to rise,
When I recall how clearly,
I saw Christ in Mother's eyes.

AN OLD-FASHIONED MOTHER

Text: I Sam. 1:9-11,24-28; 3:20.
INTRODUCTION:

In ancient Greece a day known as "mothering day," in which special gifts were given.

Early Christians adopted this as a special day of worship. Childdren carried gifts from the church to their parents.

After seven years of campaigning by Ann Jarvis, a congressional resolution was signed by President Wilson on May 8, 1914, setting aside the second Sunday of May "For the public expression of our love and reverence for the mothers."

Story of Hannah (from text)

PROPOSITION: THERE ARE IMPORTANT LESSONS TO BE LEARNED FROM THIS OLD-FASHIONED MOTHER.

I. HANNAH LOOKED UPON MOTHERHOOD AS A PRIVILEGE.
  1. When denied the privilege of motherhood she spent years in grief.
  2. She prayed earnestly that she might become a mother.
  3. One of the greatest privileges bestowed upon woman is that of motherhood.

II. HANNAH WAS A PRAYING MOTHER.
  1. "She prayed unto Jehovah, and wept sore" — 1:10.
  2. "For this child I prayed" — 1:27.
  3. Responsibility of motherhood ought to prompt earnest prayer.

III. HANNAH GAVE HER CHILD TO GOD.
  1. Her vow to God — 1:11.
  2. She prepared him for God's service while in his infancy.
  3. She brought him to the house of God.

IV. HANNAH SUCCEEDED IN THE HIGHEST OF VOCATIONS.
  1. "All Israel knew that Samuel was established to be a prophet."
  2. He was not an abnormal boy, but he had a godly mother.

3. She succeeded because of her commitment to God and her family.

CONCLUSION:

The ideal mother looks upon motherhood as a privilege, prays, gives her child to God, and succeeds in the highest of vocations.

How desperately the world needs such mothers for such a time as this.

Mothers need to be right with God to be right with their families.

TRIBUTES

The mother in her office holds the key
Of the soul; and she it is who stamps the coin
Of character and makes the being who would be a savage
But for her gentle care, a Christian man.

"There was no great man who did not have a great mother." —Olive Schreiner

"Let France have good mothers and she will have good sons." —Napoleon

"An arrow warped in the making will never be straight in its flight." —Indian proverb

"As the twig is bent the tree's inclined." —Alexander Pope

"A kiss from my mother made me a painter." —Benjamin West

"The mother's heart is the child's first school room." —Beecher

"All I am my mother made me." —John Quincy Adams

"My mother was the making of me. The memory of her will always be a blessing." —Thomas Edison

"All that I am, or ever hope to be, I owe to my angel mother."
—D.L. Moody

A PRAYER FOR MOTHERS

God give us Mothers, this we plead,
To still our woes in hours of need.
To hush with gentle accents blest,

129

The bitter cry. And soothe to rest
The weary soul. For this we pray,
To Mother's God on Mother's Day.
　　　　　—John F. Todd

MOTHER'S DAY AT THE CROSS

Text: John 19:25-27.
INTRODUCTION:
Of the many wonderful Bible mothers, Mary is outstanding.
1. She welcomed the birth of the Messiah — Luke 1:26-38.
2. She presented Him to the Lord — Luke 2:22-24.
3. She preached a powerful sermon in John 2:5.
4. She sought to keep in touch with her son — Matt. 12:46.
5. A sword pierced her soul at Calvary — Luke 2:35.
6. Jesus' last words express concern for His mother — John 19:25-27.

PROPOSITION: THERE ARE LESSONS FOR MOTHERS AND SONS AT THE CROSS.
I. THE MOTHERS' LESSON: "BEHOLD THY SON."
1. The privilege of loving.
"A kiss from my mother made me a painter" —Benjamin West.
2. The privilege of teaching.
II Tim. 1:5.
3. The privilege of example.
"Let France have good mothers and she will have good sons" —Napoleon.
II. THE SONS' LESSON: "BEHOLD THY MOTHER."
1. Honor your mother.
The first commandment with promise — Exo. 20:12.
2. Mother gave you life.
Probably sacrificed for your well-being.
3. Mother gave you home.
A little girl, when asked where her home was, replied, "Where mother is."
4. Mother gave you love.
Isa. 66:13.
CONCLUSION:
How we may honor our mothers:
1. By caring for them. "He took her to his own home."

2. By returning their love.
3. By following their example.
4. By acknowledging and accepting the God Who gave them to us.

WHAT IS A MOTHER?

A Mother can be almost any size or age, but she won't admit to being over 30. A Mother has soft hands and smells good.

A Mother likes new dresses, music, a clean house, her children's kisses, an automatic washer, and daddy.

A Mother doesn't like muddy feet, having her children sick, temper tantrums, loud noises, or a bad report card.

A Mother can read a thermometer (much to the amazement of Dad) and, like magic, can kiss away a hurt.

A Mother can bake good cakes and pies but likes to see her children eat vegetables. A Mother can stuff a baby into a snow suit in seconds and can kiss little sad faces and make them smile.

A Mother is underpaid, has long hours and gets very little rest. She worries too much about her children, but she doesn't mind it at all.

And no matter how old her children are, she still likes to think of them as her little babies. She is the guardian angel of the family, the queen, the tender hand of love.

A Mother is the best friend anyone ever had. A Mother is love. . . . God bless her.

———————

"Most of the good things in this life come to us in twos and threes, dozens and hundreds — plenty of roses, stars, sunsets, rainbows, brothers and sisters, aunts and cousins, comrades and friends — but only one Mother in all this wide, wide world."

MOTHER — DAD — AND CHILD

Text: I Sam. 1-3.

INTRODUCTION:

An Old Testament story appropriate for Mother's Day, Father's Day, Children's Day.

Relate the story of Hannah, Elkanah, and Samuel from I Samuel, chapters 1-3.

PROPOSITION: MAY MOTHERS, FATHERS, AND CHILDREN FOLLOW THE EXAMPLE OF THESE THREE BIBLE CHARACTERS.

I. THE MOTHER-SERMON EXEMPLIFIED BY HANNAH.

1. She looked upon motherhood as a privilege — 1:5-7.
2. She was a praying mother — 1:27.
3. She gave her child to the Lord — 1:22.
4. She succeeded in the highest of vocations — 3:20.

II. THE FATHER-SERMON EXEMPLIFIED BY ELKANAH.

1. He worshipped God — 1:3.
2. He loved his family — 1:5.
3. He consented to the dedication of his son — 1:23.
4. He set a good example for his family — chap. 1.

III. THE CHILD-SERMON EXEMPLIFIED BY SAMUEL.

1. He was obedient to his parents — 1:27-28.
2. He ministered in the temple — 2:18.
3. He answered God's call — 3:10.
4. He made good. He became God's faithful prophet.

CONCLUSION:

Mothers — Recognize the privilege of motherhood, devote time to prayer, give your children to God, succeed in the highest of vocations.

Fathers — Take time for worship, love the family God has given you, dedicate your children to God, set the right example.

Children — Obey your parents in the Lord, devote time to God's work, answer when He calls, make good in the work God gives you to do.

ROOTS

Mr. and Mrs. Jonathan Edwards vowed they would raise their children "unto the glory of God." They had over 1400 descendants, many of whom are still living.

Here are the statistics of the blessings which God has visited upon the Edwards family, and upon this country as a direct result of their decision to raise their children "in the nurture and admonition of the Lord."

—13 of them were college presidents
—65 of them were university professors
—100 of them were lawyers
—1 of them was the dean of a law school
—30 of them were judges
—56 of them were physicians
—80 of them ran for and held public offices
—3 of them were U.S. senators
—3 of them were governors
—1 of them was Vice-President of the U.S.
—1 of them was U.S. Treasury controller
—100 of them were missionaries
—600 of them were preachers of the gospel

Perhaps your own "roots" are just as impressive. If not, how about becoming a root yourself so that future generations will say comparable things about you and your descendants?

—News of The Way

THE MAGNIFICENT MINORITY

Text: Luke 17:11-19.

INTRODUCTION:

"Sauntering down the Jaffa Road on my approach to the holy city, in a kind of dreamy maze, with, as I remember, scarcely one distinct idea in my head, I was startled out of my reverie by the sudden apparition of a crowd of beggars, without eyes, nose, hair. They held up to me their handless arms; unearthly sounds gurgled through throats without palates. In a word, I was horrified." —Dr. Thomson.

Such was the group the Master and His disciples met on their way to Jerusalem.

Recount the story of the healing of the ten lepers: Luke 17.

PROPOSITION: LET US LEARN THE LESSON OF THANKSGIVING FROM THE HEALED LEPER.

I. IN WHAT RESPECT ARE THESE TEN ALIKE?
  1. They are all lepers. They are among the living dead.
  2. They all have faith in Jesus.
     They have enough faith to come to Him, to pray, and to follow His instructions.
  3. They are all healed — "As they went, they were cleansed."

II. IN WHAT RESPECT DO THESE TEN DIFFER?
  1. Nine are Jews, God's chosen. One is a despised Samaritan.
  2. Nine went their way. One returned to give thanks.
  3. The Samaritan was a minority, but what a magnificent minority!

III. WHY WAS ONE GRATEFUL AND NINE UNGRATEFUL?
  1. Perhaps nine had never developed the grateful habit.
  2. Perhaps nine were so absorbed in the gift they forgot the giver.
  3. Perhaps nine considered other things more important than giving thanks.

IV. WHAT RESULTED FROM GRATITUDE — AND INGRATITUDE?

135

1. By ingratitude they robbed themselves. We lose something vital when we lose a sense of gratitude. They also robbed themselves of fellowship with the Master.
2. By ingratitude they robbed others.
3. By gratitude the Samaritan was blest and the Master's heart was gladdened. The Samaritan received spiritual wholeness as well as physical.

CONCLUSION:

Thanksgiving is not a day; it is a habit.

You can not be thankful on Thanksgiving unless you have been learning how all year.

Will you find your place today with the wise Samaritan and join him in the high service of praise?

THINKING ABOUT THANKSGIVING

Matthew Henry, the famous Bible Scholar and commentator, was once accosted by thieves and robbed of his purse. The following words were penned in his diary: "Let me thankful first because I was never robbed before; second, although they took my purse, they did not take my life; third, because although they took my all, it was not much; and fourth, because it was I who was robbed, not I who robbed."

———

Thanksgiving is good — Thanksliving is better.

———

There is not a hearth so bleak and bare
But heaven hath sent some blessing there;
No table e'er so sparsely spread
But that a grace should there be said;
No life but knows some moment blest
Of sweet contentment and of rest;
No heart so cold but heaven above
Hath touched it with the warmth of love.

136

So count your blessings, one by one,
At early morn or set of sun,
And like an incense, to the skies
Your prayers of thankfulness shall rise.
Look for the love that heaven sends,
That good that every soul intends;
Thus you will learn the only way
To keep a true Thanksgiving Day.

———

"Beggar that I am, I am poor even in thanks." —Shakespeare

———

When the Sunday School teacher asked her class what they were thankful for, one little fellow replied, "My glasses. They keep the boys from fighting me and the girls from kissing me!"

WHEN JESUS SAID "THANKS"

Texts: Rom. 1:10-23; Psa. 107:15.

INTRODUCTION:

19 centuries ago lived one who, according to our standards, had very little for which he might be thankful.

1. He was born in a stable and laid in a manger.
2. His boyhood was spent in a carpenter shop in a hill town.
3. He never owned a home or had a family.
4. He was an outcast to His brethren.
5. For three and one-half years He was an itinerant preacher.
6. He died not owning six feet of ground in which to be buried.
7. Yet "He lifted up his eyes, and said, Father, I thank thee. . . ."

PROPOSITION: MAY JESUS' THANKSGIVING BE AN EXAMPLE TO US.

I. JESUS SAID "THANK YOU" FOR MATERIAL BLESSINGS — John 6:11.
   1. The blessing and multiplying of a lad's lunch.
   2. Every material gift is from above — James 1:17; Phil. 4:19.
   3. Have we said "Thank you" for things?

II. JESUS SAID "THANK YOU" FOR COMMUNION WITH GOD — John 11:41.
   1. The occasion of this prayer — John 11:31-41.
   2. When we come to Him in faith, He "hears" us — John 14:13-14.
   3. Have we said "Thank you" for the privilege of prayer?

III. JESUS SAID "THANK YOU" FOR THE PLAN AND PROVIDENCE OF THE FATHER — Luke 10:21.
   1. The mysteries of the Kingdom are given to "babes."
   2. The Creator has a plan for the world, the church, and the individual.
   3. Have we said "Thank you" for the providence of God?

IV. JESUS SAID "THANK YOU" FOR OPPORTUNITIES OF SERVICE AND SACRIFICE — Matt. 26:26-28.

1. The blessing of the loaf and cup, but more.
2. The institution of the Lord's Supper. Jesus' last night upon earth. His greatest sacrifice was on hand.
3. Have we said "Thank you" for opportunities of service and sacrifice? Matt. 16:24.

CONCLUSION:

Jesus' life of thanksgiving ought to be our example.

On this Thanksgiving Day may we thank God for His provision, for His nearness, for His plan, and for the privilege of serving and sacrificing for Him.

GIVING THANKS

A little strength was lost each day,
A little hope dropped by the way,
The feet dragged slowly up the road,
The shoulders bent beneath their load,
Courage seemed dying in the heart,
the will played but a feeble part.
     Night brought no ease,
     Day no surcease,
From heavy cares or wearying smart,
     Then, why give thanks?

Somehow, strength lasted through the day,
Hope joined with courage in the way;
The feet still kept the uphill road,
The shoulders did nor drop their load;
An unseen power sustained the heart
When flesh and will failed in their part,
     While God gave light
     By day and night,
And also grace to bear the smart.
     For this give thanks.

139

Thanks for the daily bread which feeds
The body's wants, the spirit's needs;
Thanks for the keen, the quick'ning word,
"He only lives who lives in God,"
Whether his time on earth is spent
In lordly house or labor's tent.
    Thanks for the light
      By day and night,
Which shows the way the Master went.
    And He gave thanks.

THANKFUL — FOR WHAT?

Text: Psa. 103:1-5.

INTRODUCTION:

Illus: A man, looking at a notice in a post office window, stating, "Closed for Thanksgiving Day," was heard to mutter, "Thankful — for what?"

Ingratitude is one of the most hurtful and hurting of sins.

When we lose a sense of thankfulness we lose something vital to life.

We might think David had little for which to be thankful. Recount his hardships . . . but David praised God for His benefits.

In Psalm 103 David selects a few pearls from the casket of divine love, threads them on the string of memory, and hangs them about the neck of gratitude.

PROPOSITION: PSALM 103 LISTS BENEFITS FOR WHICH WE SHOULD BLESS JEHOVAH.

I. FORGIVENESS — "Who forgiveth all thine iniquities."
1. If only some sins were forgiven we would be as bad off as before.
2. His forgiveness is complete — Psa. 103:12.

II. HEALING — "Who healeth all thy diseases."
1. All healing is of God, whether wrought through prayer, medicine, surgery, or mental suggestion. God is the healer.
2. There is a greater healing — James 5:14-15.

III. REDEMPTION — "Who redeemeth thy life from destruction."
1. Redeemed: "To buy back." — I Pet. 1:18-19.
2. If bought, where is the title to your life? I Cor. 6:19-20.

IV. CORONATION — "Who crowneth thee with lovingkindness and tender mercies."
1. Not just kindness, but "lovingkindness." Not just mercies, but "tender mercies."
2. Shall He crown us and we not crown Him? "Crown Him Lord of all."

V. SATISFACTION — "Who satisfieth thy desire with good things."
1. "No good thing will he withhold" — Psa. 84:11.
2. He is able to satisfy every need — Phil. 4:19.

VI. REGENERATION — "So that thy youth is renewed."
1. Life begins when man meets Jesus — II Cor. 5:17.
2. Eternal life is our present possession.

CONCLUSION:
For what are you thankful this Thanksgiving Day? (Recap.)
"Beware lest thou forget Jehovah" — Deut. 6:10-12.

RECESSIONAL

A six-year-old boy tip-toed to the crib of his baby brother. His face was grave, but his eyes were shining, as he whispered, "Baby brother, tell me all about God before you forget."

God of our fathers, known of old —
   Lord of our far-flung battle line —
Beneath whose awful hand we hold
   Dominion over palm and pine —
Lord God of Hosts, be with us yet;
Lest we forget — lest we forget!

The tumult and the shouting dies —
   The Captains and the Kings depart —
Still stands thine ancient sacrifice,
   An humble and a contrite heart.
Lord God of hosts, be with us yet;
Lest we forget — lest we forget!

Far-called, our navies melt away —
   On dune and headland sinks the fire —
Lo, all our pomp of yesterday
   Is one with Nineveh and Tyre!
Judge of the nations, spare us yet —
Lest we forget — lest we forget!

THANKFUL — FOR WHAT?

If, drunk with sight of power, we lose
  Wild tongues that have not Thee in awe —
Such boastings as the Gentiles use.
  Or lesser breeds without the law —
Lord God of hosts, be with us yet;
Lest we forget — lest we forget!

—Rudyard Kipling

THE GREATEST GIFT

Text: John 3:16
INTRODUCTION:
> Christmas has become a time for giving and receiving gifts.
> Of the many costly gifts, what is the greatest ever given? How appropriately the Golden Text of the Bible should define this gift.
> Paul endeavored to describe the Greatest Gift in II Cor. 9:15. A word used only once in the Bible: *anekdiegeto* — indescribable, unspeakable.

> It was unspeakable LOVE that thought it.
> It was an unspeakable LIFE that brought it.
> It was an unspeakable DEATH that wrought it.
> It is unspeakable JOY when taught it.

PROPOSITION: SEE THE NATURE OF THE GREATEST GIFT AND RESPOND.
>   I. IT WAS A DIVINE GIFT: "GOD so loved the world."
>   The value of a gift is partially determined by the giver.
>   II. IT WAS A LOVE GIFT: "God SO LOVED the world."
>   The value of a gift is not measured so much in dollars and cents as in the heart of the giver.
>   III. IT WAS A UNIVERSAL GIFT: "God so loved THE WORLD."
>   The only world-wide gift ever given.
>   "Great joy which shall be to ALL the people" — Luke 2:10.
>   IV. IT WAS AN UNEARNED GIFT: "God so loved . . . that HE GAVE."
>   No man was deserving of such a gift.
>   This is the meaning of grace — "unmerited favor" — John 1:14.
>   V. IT WAS A PRICELESS GIFT: "HIS ONLY BEGOTTEN SON."
>   Many things God might have given: wealth, health, ease.

God gave what man needed, not what he wanted.
VI. IT WAS A PERSONAL GIFT: "That WHOSOEVER believeth."
The greatest Christmas gift bears your name: "Whosoever."
God prepared your gift and placed it on a tree — I Pet. 2:24.
VII. IT WAS AN ETERNAL GIFT: "EVERLASTING LIFE."
Some gifts become broken; some tarnish; some wear out.
This gift grows brighter with age. It improves with the using. It is sufficient for this world and that which is to come.
CONCLUSION:
Have you received your gift, or have you left it waiting at the tree?
1. Wise men offered gifts and fell down and worshipped.
2. Wise men returned to their own country another way.
3. Shepherds made known what they had seen and heard. They came and saw — They went and told.

A LIVING GIFT

He did not use a silvery box
 Or paper green and red;
God laid His Christmas gift to men
 Within a manger bed.

No silken cord was used to bind
 The gift sent from above.
'Twas wrapped in swaddling clothes and bound
 In cords of tender love.

There was no evergreen to which
 His precious gift was tied;
Upon a bare tree on a hill,
 His gift was hung . . . and died.

'Twas taken down from off the tree
And laid within the sod,
But death itself could not destroy
The precious gift of God.

With mighty hand He lifted it
From out the stony grave;
Forevermore to every man
A living gift He gave.

—Ruth Prentice

"He who does not have Christmas in his heart will never find it under a tree."

"A Christless Christmas is pretty much like a counterfeit dollar."

"Presents under the Christmas tree are of less importance than the presence of Christ in our hearts."

146

WHAT ARE YOU GIVING FOR CHRISTMAS?

Text: Matt. 2:11.
INTRODUCTION:
>Wise men brought gifts to Jesus. How appropriate and significant their gifts. They gave their very best.
>Children anticipate what they will "get" for Christmas. As we mature we think more of what we may give.

>If we lived Christmas each day as we should
>And made it our aim to always do good,
>We'd find the lost key to meaningful living
>That comes not from Getting but from unselfish Giving.

>—Helen Steiner Rice

PROPOSITION: WHAT SHALL WE GIVE FOR CHRISTMAS?
>II. TO THE NEEDY — MAY WE GIVE A HELPING HAND.
>I John 3:17.
>"A helping hand is a heart with fingers."
>II. TO THE SORROWING — MAY WE GIVE COMFORT.
>Isa. 40:1.
>Let the sorrowing know that the star of hope is still shining.
>III. TO THE DISHEARTENED — MAY WE GIVE HOPE.
>For many the star of hope has become tarnished.
>**Illus:** Jesus restored disheartened Thomas — John 20.
>IV. TO THE LONELY — MAY WE GIVE FRIENDSHIP.
>There are many "lonely people in the city."
>Some lonely because they have fallen away — Gal. 6:1.
>V. TO OUR ENEMIES — MAY WE GIVE FORGIVENESS.
>Matt. 5:23-24.
>Lay aside those heavy grudges when Christmas comes.
>VI. TO THE NON-CHRISTIAN — MAY WE GIVE THE SAVIOUR.
>For multitudes this will be Christmas without Christ.
>There can be no greater gift — Matt. 2:11.

147

VII. TO GOD — MAY WE GIVE OUR HEARTS.
Clean out the rooms — open the doors — make room for Jesus.
"Come into my heart, Lord Jesus; there's room in my heart for Thee."
CONCLUSION:
Matt. 2:11.
What shall I give for Christmas? Recap.
Fall down before Him, present your gifts, and you can join the heavenly anthem, "Glory to God in the highest. . . ."

PATTERN OF LOVE

I didn't question Timmy, age nine, or his seven-year-old brother Billy about the brown wrapping paper they passed back and forth between them as we visited each store.

Every year at Christmas time, our Service Club takes the children from poor families in our town on a personally conducted shopping tour. I was assigned Timmy and Billy, whose father was out of work. After giving them the alloted $4 each, we began our trip. At different stores I made suggestions, but always their answer was a solemn shake of the head, "no." Finally I asked, "Where would you suggest we look?"

"Could we go to a shoe store, Sir?" answered Timmy. "We'd like a pair of shoes for our Daddy so he can go to work."

In the shoe store the clerk asked what the boys wanted. Out came the brown paper. "We want a pair of work shoes to fit this foot," they said. Billy explained that it was a pattern of their Daddy's foot. They had drawn it while he was asleep in a chair.

The clerk held the paper against a measuring stick, then walked away. Soon, he came with an open box. "Will these do?" he asked.

Timmy and Billy handled the shoes with great eagerness. "How much do they cost?" asked Billy.

Then Timmy saw the price on the box. "They're $16.95," he said in dismay. "We only have $8."

I looked at the clerk and he cleared his throat. "That's the regular

148

price," he said, "but they're on sale; $3.98, today only."

Then, with shoes happily in hand, the boys bought gifts for their mother, and two little sisters. Not once did they think of themselves.

The day after Christmas the boy's father stopped me in the street. The new shoes were on his feet, gratitude was in his eyes. "I just thank Jesus for people who care," he said.

"And I thank Jesus for your two sons," I replied. "They taught me more about Christmas in one evening than I had learned in a lifetime."

—Jack Smith, as told to Raymond Knowles

A PERFECT CHRISTMAS

Text: Matt. 2:10-12.
INTRODUCTION:

Jewish expectancy linked the coming of Messiah to a star — Num. 24:17. Messiah-Haggadah and Midrashim foretold appearance of a star.

Wise-men from the East saw and followed a star.

In Bethlehem they experienced a perfect Christmas.

PROPOSITION: MAY YOU EXPERIENCE ALL ELEMENTS OF A PERFECT CHRISTMAS.

I. IT WAS A DAY OF JOY — v. 10.

  1. Those who missed the star missed the joy.
  2. They rejoiced because of divine presence and guidance.
  3. Christmas is not perfect without joy — I Pet. 1:8.

II. IT WAS A DAY OF WORSHIP — v. 11a.

  1. This was the purpose of their quest — v. 2.
  2. They completed their quest. They fell down and worshipped.
  3. Christmas is not perfect without worship.

III. IT WAS A DAY OF GIVING — v. 11b.

  1. Their gifts were useful and prophetic.
  2. Their gifts were acceptable because they first presented themselves.
  3. Christmas is not perfect without giving.
     Our gifts to Him can be bestowed upon others.

IV. IT WAS A DAY OF OBEDIENCE — v. 12.

  1. Herod commanded, "Bring me word." They obeyed God rather than man.
  2. They went back another way.
     How can we go on in the way of the world after we have opened our treasure at the feet of Jesus?
  3. Christmas is not perfect without obedience.

CONCLUSION:

You will experience a perfect Christmas if you follow the wise-men.

150

A PERFECT CHRISTMAS

1. Behold the star with joy unspeakable.
2. Fall down and open your treasure before Him.
3. Go back a different way.

Make this Christmas a time of joy, worship, giving, and obedience and you will experience a perfect Christmas.

WHY HE CAME

The Christ of Christmas did not come because men were seeking God, but because God was seeking men.

The Bethlehem Babe was truly the Son of God. Herod could not destroy Him; the grave could not hold Him. He is proclaimed of God, acknowledged by angels, adored by saints, and feared by devils. What place does He have in your life?

HAVE YOU ROOM?

Have you room in your heart for a tiny Babe
Who came to earth last night,
When the inns were too filled with the worldly things
To make room for a helpless Mite?

Ah, the Christmas stars were like sudden tears
As Joseph and Mary went by
To a lowly stable in Bethlehem,
While the angels watched from on high.

Let us open our hearts to the Child today,
And who knows — the old world may thrill
When the angels sing, as they sang of old,
"Peace on Earth to Men of Good Will!"

If we can keep Christmas for a day, why can't we keep it all year?

WHEN GOD CAME ALIVE

Text: John 1:14.
INTRODUCTION:

God has always been alive, but in a stable in Bethlehem He came alive in human flesh.

Illus: Mother, comforting her little girl during a severe storm, said, "Don't be afraid; God is always near." The little one replied, "I know God is always near, but when the thunder and lightning is so bad I want someone near who has skin on them."

We reverently acknowledge that Jesus is God in the flesh.

PROPOSITION: WHEN HAPPENED WHEN GOD CAME ALIVE.

I. GOD'S WORD WAS VINDICATED.
   1. Throughout the Old Testament God promised to send the Messiah. Gen. 3:15; Gen. 12:3; Isa. 7:14; Isa. 9:6; Micah 5:2.
   2. When God came alive this prophetic word was vindicated.

II. GOD'S CHARACTER WAS ILLUSTRATED.
   1. Man knew little of God's character before the incarnation — John 1:18.
   2. The only perfect revelation God ever made of Himself was made through Jesus Christ — John 14:7-9.

III. GOD'S LOVE WAS DEMONSTRATED.
   1. God's love was manifested in giving His Son — I John 4:9.
   2. The value of a gift is measured by the heart of the giver — John 3:16.

IV. GOD'S PURPOSE WAS CONSUMMATED.
   1. God's purpose since the inception of sin was to redeem His lost creation — Gal. 4:4-5.
   2. The incarnation begins the final chapter in the consummation of His purpose.

   Calvary, not Bethlehem, is the place of redemption — Heb. 9:26; I Pet. 1:18-19.

   He bore our sins in His body upon the tree — I Pet. 2:24.

152

CONCLUSION:
   All of this happened when God came alive.
   The Christmas story is wonderful, but the message of Christmas is incomplete until God comes alive in your heart.

   O Holy Child of Bethlehem!
   Descend to us, we pray;
   Cast out our sin,
   And enter in;
   Be born in us today.

O LITTLE TOWN OF BETHLEHEM

I shall always remember Bethlehem.

As we travel down those barren slopes along the winding road from Jerusalem, it is altogether fitting that we come first to a home for little children. Then, as we round a gentle curve, spread out before us is the panorama of Bethlehem: grey stone, flat-roofed buildings, with church spires outlining the horizon and, stretching out below us, the Shepherds' Fields.

Entering the city though the narrow, shop-lined streets, we approach the Church of the Nativity and Manger Square. Stooping to pass through a doorway at the rear of the court yard, we descend worn stone steps to the grotto which is the traditional site of the stable. Here is the manger and the star on the floor which supposedly marks the spot of the Messiah's birth. In the candle-lit cavern we bow and sing, "Silent Night! Holy Night!" and worship Him Who was born there so long ago.

Perhaps you may never be privileged to stand there in the flesh but you, too, can bow down and worship Him Who was born Christ the Lord.

PLAYING THE GAME

Text: Heb. 12:1-2.

INTRODUCTION:

Most young people enjoy games, both as spectators and participants.

The apostle Paul was a sports fan.

While in Rome he must have witnessed the games. Many references to sports events in his writings. I Cor. 9:24-27; II Tim. 4:7-8; Heb. 12:1-2.

PROPOSITION: BE CHALLENGED TO PLAY THE GAME OF LIFE WELL.

I. THE PREPARATION: "Lay aside every weight."

Can not play the game well if encumbered by weight.

Weights to lay aside: Gal. 5:19-21.

There is no time lost in making adequate preparation.

II. THE PARTICIPANTS: "Let us."

The game of life is played by all.

Do not all have the same abilities. What will you do with what you have?

III. THE SPECTATORS: "So great a cloud of witnesses."

list the cloud of witnesses in Heb. 11. Our examples.

The spectators encourage us to play up to our potential.

IV. THE GAME: "The race that is set before us."

Don't sit on the side-lines. Get into the race!

Play the game! Play it clean! Play it fair! Play your best! Play to the last whistle!

V. THE GOAL: "Looking unto Jesus."

Paul had seen the runners straining toward the goal and receiving the laurel crown.

II Tim. 4:7-8.

A battle to fight —
A race to run —
A faith to keep —
A crown to receive.

CONCLUSION:
   Only one game to play — play it well.
   Only one life to live — live it well.

   Play the game.
   Play it fair.
   Play it clean.
   Play it to the end.
   Play it with Christ.

FINISHING THE COURSE

The queen of track meets is the Olympic Games, which are held every four years. Many thrilling and memorable events have occurred during these competitions. One of the most thrilling and remarkable occurred during the 1932 games in California.

The time had arrived for the 5,000 meter race. That is more than three miles, and it is a difficult event. As the race was about to begin all eyes were on the Finns, who had a reputation as distance runners. But, as the race progressed, attention was diverted to a diminutive figure who dropped further and further behind the other runners. The small Japanese boy was badly outclassed.

After several laps it looked as though the runner would be unable to complete the race, but he would reach down for a bit more energy, put on a burst of speed, then fall even further back.

When the leaders crossed the finish line the Japanese lad was right there with them — but an entire lap behind! Everyone but the little oriental thought that the race was over. He had different ideas; he had come to run a race so, all alone, he continued around the track. A mighty roar arose from the throats of 80,000 spectators as they stood to their feet and applauded until the runner crossed the line and collapsed on the grass. Who can say that he was not a winner? He was glorious in defeat. He finished the course.

155

SMOOTH STONES TO SLAY GIANTS

Text: I Sam. 17:40; I Tim. 4:12.
INTRODUCTION:

Portray the story of the champion and the shepherd boy — I Sam. 17.

The giant "disdained him; for he was but a youth" — I Sam. 17:42.

David chose 5 smooth stones to slay the giant.

Many centuries passed, and an old preacher writes to a young preacher, "Let no man despise thy youth," then gives 5 stones that are giant killers.

PROPOSITION: OUR TEXT LISTS 5 SMOOTH STONES WITH WHICH YOUNG PEOPLE CAN SLAY GIANTS.

  I. AN EXAMPLE IN WORD.

Illus: In physical examination doctor says, "Stick out your tongue." Physical and spiritual condition can be ascertained from the tongue.

Are your words those that would slay giants?

 II. AN EXAMPLE IN MANNER OF LIFE.

The Christian life is the "different" life — Rom. 12:2.

Refusal to be different brings sorrow and loss of witness — Rom. 2:24.

Your life can be a giant killer.

III. AN EXAMPLE IN LOVE.

The new commandment — John 13:34-35.

Said of early Christians: "Behold, how they love one another."

Love for God and man can slay giants.

 IV. AN EXAMPLE IN FAITH.

Faith is the foundation of our salvation — Acts 16:31.

Faith makes us overcomers — I John 4:4; 5:4.

By faith we serve and reach out to others.

  V. AN EXAMPLE IN PURITY.

Don't be an ivory soap Christian: 99 44/100% pure.

Living in a time when it is not easy to remain pure.

It is the call of the difficult, but the way that brings victory and joy, and the way that wins.

CONCLUSION:

Does the world disdain you because you are a youth, or is your life such that "no man despises your youth?"

Five smooth stones are available to you. Use them! Be a giant killer for God!

WRESTLING FOR GOD

It was the days of the Roman legions. To be a Roman soldier was the acme of physical perfection. The soldiers were trained rigorously in the games, wrestling, and combat.

Disturbing tidings reached the ears of the Emperor. It was rumored that the teachings of the Nazarene had infiltrated the ranks of his legions. The army was assembled and the command given: "Let those who call themselves Christians step forward. Forty men broke the ranks and stepped out for Christ. The edict was sounded: "Renounce Christ or die." Forty soldiers responded, "We choose Christ!"

The Christian soldiers were marched through the snow to an ice-covered lake, stripped of their armor and their clothing, and marched onto the ice to renounce Christ or die. They were told that when they were ready to renounce Christ they could return to the fire and be reinstated in the ranks.

The forty men turned their backs on the fire and marched onto the sea of ice. As they marched, they took up the chant, "Forty wrestlers, wrestling for God, claiming for Thee, Oh Christ, the victory, and from Thee the crown."

The numbing cold ate its way into the bodies of the martyrs. Finally one of them could stand it no longer and returned to the fire. The remaining heroes took up the chant, "Thirty-nine wrestlers, wrestling for God. . . ."

The refrain beat time and time again in the ears of the commanding officer. Unable to stand it longer, he cried out, "If that is Christianity, I, too, am a Christian." He laid aside his armor, stripped off

157

his clothing, turned his back on the fire, marched out to join the martyrs, and they once more took up their cry of victory:

> "Forty wrestlers, wrestling for God, claiming for Thee, Oh Christ, the victory, and from Thee the crown."

IN QUEST OF SUCCESS

Text: Acts 1:10-14.
INTRODUCTION:
    All are interested in becoming successful, but what is success?
    "The progressive realization of a worthy ideal."
    The Book of Acts tells the story of eleven men who found success. They were not likely candidates: common Galileans, fishermen. None would have been voted most likely to succeed. Yet the world has never forgotten these eleven men.
PROPOSITION: THE SECRET OF SUCCESS IS REVEALED IN THE FIRST CHAPTER OF ACTS.
  I. THEY WERE LOOKING UP — v. 10.
    1. Don't go through life with your head down.
    Those with their eyes on the ground see no angels.
    2. Look up — set goals that are high and worthy.
    3. Success was not found in the goal alone.
 II. THEY RETURNED TO PREPARE — vs. 12-14.
    1. Success never comes to the unprepared.
    There is no time lost by preparation.
    2. The nature of their preparation — v. 14.
    3. Success was not found in preparation alone.
III. THEY WENT OUT TO SERVE.
    1. The Book of Acts is the record of dedicated service.
    2. They preached the gospel, healed the sick, comforted the sorrowing, won souls to Jesus Christ.
    They never became too great to do the little things.
    3. It was in service that they found success.
CONCLUSION:
    How shall we measure success? Two criteria:
    1. The world's answer: "Success is determined by the things you take out of the world for yourself."
    2. Christ's answer: "Success is determined by the amount of your life that you invest in a needy world."
    Which way will you choose? It is service that measures success.

SUCCESS

It isn't the cut of the clothes that you wear,
  Nor the stuff out of which they are made,
Though chosen with taste and fastidious care.
  And it isn't the price that you paid;
It isn't the size of your pile in the bank,
  Nor the number of acres you own;
It isn't a question of prestige or rank,
  Nor of sinew and muscle and bone;
It isn't the servants that come at your call,
  It isn't the things you possess,
Whether many or little — or nothing at all —
  It's service that measures success.

It isn't a question of name or of length
  Of an ancestral pedigree,
Nor a question of mental vigor and strength,
  Nor a question of social degree;
It isn't a question of city or town ,
  Nor a question of doctrine or creed;
It isn't a question of fame or renown,
  Nor a question of valorous deed;
But he who makes someone happy each day,
  And he who gives heed to distress,
Will find satisfaction the richest of pay,
  For it's service that measures success.

"Service is the rent we owe mankind for the space we occupy here on the earth — yet a surprising number of professing Christians never get religion in their hands and feet."

"A helping hand is a heart with fingers."

WHEN THEY MET THE MASTER

Text: Luke 19:1.

INTRODUCTION:

    A thrill to meet great individuals. Their influence on our lives.

    Many met Jesus during His earthly sojourn. He brought many changes.

    Luke 19:1. He was "passing through." He will not force Himself on any. Zacchaeus was determined to see Him. Life was changed.

    Anxious that every young person meet Jesus, for life is never the same after you meet Him.

PROPOSITION: SEE WHAT HAPPENS WHEN YOUNG PEOPLE MEET JESUS.

   I. A RICH YOUNG RULER — Mark 10:17-22.

      1. He was earnest, anxious, respectful, religious, but unwilling to pay the price of discipleship.

      2. To him Jesus was a DISAPPOINTMENT. He went away sorrowful.

  II. TWO YOUNG MEN IN A BOAT — Matt. 4:21-22.

      1. Two hot-headed young fishermen (nicknamed "Boanerges" — sons of thunder).

      They were transformed. One wrote, "Be patient unto the coming of the Lord." The other penned, "Beloved, let us love one another."

      2. To them Jesus meant TRANSFORMED LIVES.

 III. A YOUNG MAN ON A CROSS — Luke 23:40-43.

      1. Not certain he was "young," but he was not hardened by sin.

      He had never set out as Calvary for his goal. Somewhere he missed the mark and became a common criminal. He recognized Jesus, saluted Him as King, and found pardon.

      2. To him Jesus was HIS SAVIOUR.

 IV. A YOUNG MAN NAMED SAUL — Acts 7:58; 9:1-22.

      1. A brilliant, highly educated, zealous Jew.

      Persecuter of Christians, but he never forgot the testimony

161

of Stephen — Acts 22:20.

2. To him Jesus was a LIFE WORK.
    Be a member of the "6:8 Club" (Isa. 6:1-8).
CONCLUSION:
    Jesus entered and was passing through Jericho. Jesus has
    entered and is passing through your home town.
    Meet Him, invite Him in. Life is never the same after meeting
    Jesus.

WHEN I MET THE MASTER

I had walked life's way with an easy tread,
Had followed where comforts or pleasure led.
Until one day, in a quiet place,
I met the Master, face to face.

With station and rank and wealth for my goal,
Much for my body, but none for my soul;
I had entered to win in life's big race
When I met the Master, face to face.

I had built my castles and reared them high,
With their towers had pierced to the blue of the sky;
I had sworn to rule with an iron mace
When I met the Master, face to face.

I met Him; I knew Him; and blushed to see
That His eyes, full of sorrow, were fixed on me,
And I faltered and fell at His feet that day,
While my castles melted and vanished away.

Melted and vanished, and in their place
Naught else could I see but my Saviour's face,
And I cried aloud, "Oh make me meet
To follow the steps of thy wounded feet!"

My thought is now for the souls of men,
I have lost my life to find it again,
E'er since that day, in a quiet place,
When I met the Master face to face.